A Representation of Nationhood in the Museum

A Representation of Nationhood in the Museum examines how the National Museum of Korea, as a national repository of material culture and the state's premier exhibition facility, has shaped and been shaped by Korean nationalism.

Exploring the processes by which the museum has discovered and interpreted material culture, using concepts of ethnic nationalism in the historical and political contexts of South Korean society, the book analyses how this nationalist interpretation has regulated South Koreans' understanding of their material culture. Issues considered include: cultural and political relations with China; Japanese colonial rule, cultural imperialism and its legacy; the division of Korea since 1945; the Korean War and nation building since liberation in 1945; and domestic political upheavals, including military coups in 1961 and in 1979. Demonstrating that authoritarian regimes' emphasis on the promotion of national unity drove national museums to establish national identity through material culture, Jang argues that international political and diplomatic factors also affect the process of the formation of national identity in a specific political context.

Concerning itself with issues such as the relationship between politics and identity, museums and authoritarian regimes, this book should be essential reading for academics, researchers and postgraduate students in museum studies, nationalism studies, Asian studies and history departments.

Sang-hoon Jang is a curator at the National Museum of Korea. Dr. Jang completed a PhD at the University of Leicester in 2015.

Routledge Research on Museums and Heritage in Asia

Titles include

Heritage Politics in China
The Power of the Past
Yujie Zhu and Christina Maags

A Representation of Nationhood in the Museum
Sang-hoon Jang

Chinese Heritage Sites and Their Audiences
The Power of the Past
Rouran Zhang

Sacred Heritage in Japan
UNESCO, Culture, and the Changing Shape of Japanese Religion
Edited by Aike P. Rots and Mark Teeuwen

https://www.routledge.com/Routledge-Research-on-Museums-and-Heritage-in-Asia/book-series/RRMHA

A Representation of Nationhood in the Museum

Sang-hoon Jang

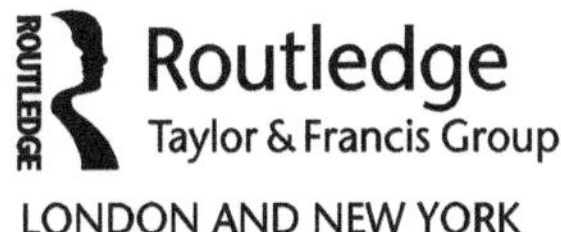

LONDON AND NEW YORK

First published 2020 by Routledge

2 Park Square, Milton Park, Abingdon, Oxon OX14 4RN
605 Third Avenue, New York, NY 10017

Routledge is an imprint of the Taylor & Francis Group, an informa business

First issued in paperback 2021

Publisher's Note

The publisher has gone to great lengths to ensure the quality of this reprint but points out that some imperfections in the original copies may be apparent.

British Library Cataloguing-in-Publication Data
A catalogue record for this book is available from the British Library

Library of Congress Cataloging-in-Publication Data
A catalog record has been requested for this book

ISBN: 978-1-138-36746-3 (hbk)
ISBN: 978-1-03-217552-2 (pbk)
DOI: 10.4324/9780429424090

Typeset in Times
by Deanta Global Publishing Services, Chennai, India

For my parents.
Jang Taek-jae (1921–2004)
and
Choi Eul-jun (1925–2012)

Contents

Figures

Tables

Acknowledgements

My special thanks go to my supervisor Professor Simon Knell for his invaluable guidance and encouragement during and after my graduate studies. I owe a particular debt to professors Hong Seung-ki, Lee Jong-wook and the late Chung Doo-hee for their advice and support since I entered Sogang University 33 years ago. I am also grateful to professors Yi Kun-moo and Bae Kidong for their special encouragement. I must thank Professors Kim Lena and Kim Youngna for their kind support. I also want to thank the three anonymous reviewers for their appreciation of my research and their insightful comments on my manuscript. My nieces Joanne Yeo and Aya Jang deserves special mention for reading my manuscript. Finally, I owe my greatest debt to my family; my mother in law Park Min-ja, Jang Hye-seung, Jang Jong-ku, Dr Jang Jong-dae, Jang Jong-wook. And a special thanks to my wife Hwang Jiyoung and our daughter Yunseo for their patience, support and love.

Abbreviations

GGM	Government-General Museum
NMK	National Museum of Korea
USAMGIK	United States Army Military Government in Korea
YHM	Yi Royal Household Museum

Introduction

In 2005, the National Museum of Korea (hereafter NMK), which was established right after the liberation from the 35-year-long Japanese colonial rule in 1945, displayed its accomplishments from the previous 60 years in building the cultural identity of Korea by opening an enormous new building located in the centre of the capital, Seoul. The then president Roh Moo-hyun (in office from 2003 to 2008) said in his congratulatory address,

> Our ethnic nation has created a proud tradition of 5000 years. ... This new museum will be a symbol to show our pride as a civilised ethnic nation. ... At the very site of military posts of foreign forces such as China, Japan and the US, this new museum building will stand tall as the centre of self-respect of our ethnic nation, proving our history and culture.[1]

These words encapsulated the manner in which NMK had become the embodiment of the discourse of ethnic national culture that Koreans strived to build both at home and abroad, using material culture.

This nationalist discourse contributed to promoting national unity and constructing the South Korean state, strongly influencing the formation of national cultural institutes like NMK. Thus, the concept of the ethnic nation has almost become the only perspective with which to discover and interpret Korean material culture, discouraging interest in other perspectives.[2] As a result, diversity and differences tend to be unexplored for the reason that they hinder the idea of national unity, while the distinct characteristics of Korean ethnic national culture tend to be overemphasised, with the goal of obtaining international recognition.[3] This tendency has restricted somewhat the possibility of diverse interpretations of cultural heritage using various criteria.

These criteria represent various identities that a categorical identification of the ethnic nation, whether intentionally or not, put aside. As Duara

(1995, p. 8) points out, "Nationalism and its theory seek a privileged position within the representational network as the master identity that subsumes or organises other identifications." However, Duara does not agree with unilateral victory of national identity, proposing to "view the dynamics of national identity within this fluid network of representations." During the past two decades, as South Korean society has seen the growth of political freedom and improvement of human rights, some South Korean academics have discussed the necessity of dissolving this adherence to national historical discourse, and have begun to disclose agendas or identities that this discourse has concealed, such as issues of gender, ethnicity and class.[4] These scholars can be said to be undertaking the task of securing more balanced perspectives not least taking disadvantaged groups and minorities, hidden behind the curtain of national discourse into consideration, in order to rediscover intentionally concealed identifications.

This research has been inspired by this new perspective, in which various identities or those representations in South Korean society should draw enough attention and secure their rightful position. In this regard, examining how the national identity of South Korea has been constructed by nationalist dynamics is important in understanding the background of the ways in which other representations of identities have been marginalised or excluded, as well as in recognising the concrete historical process and context in which the ethnic national representation was built through material culture at national cultural institutions, such as in the national museum.

The pursuit of a firm national identity played an important role in obtaining people's consent in setting the national goal and deciding which methods to utilise. This is because national identity could somehow explain why the people should unite under the direction of the nation-state. In this regard, it is interesting that authoritarian regimes in South Korea aspired to resort to the national identity, emphasising "the subjectivity of the nation" as a powerful political slogan. This means that the pursuit of national identity was closely related to the process or means by which the regime was able to secure political and moral hegemony within the national community. This also explains why these regimes were keen on taking the lead in constructing national identity by inventing and imagining various national representations. It is also interesting to consider what roles academics and museum curators played in this process.

The construction of national identity by the authoritarian regimes contributed to nationalising South Korean society, as well as providing the regimes with political and moral authority. During this period, national identity was deeply internalised by South Korean nationals. Although researchers tend to focus on criticising the political or malicious intentions behind pursuing national identity, such as justification of dictatorships, it should not be overlooked that the construction of national identity, and people's internalisation of it, have deeply influenced the formation of the South Korean modern nation-state. This government-led project also involved the participation of academics and intellectuals, as they considered the construction of the South Korean state and its national identity to be their urgent mission as well.

In this regard, it is useful to remember their occasional resistance to the dictatorship of the regimes did not necessarily mean that they were objecting to the project of constructing national identity. Rather, the project contributed to recovering the regimes' authority impaired by their dictatorships. This may explain why President Park Chung Hee (in office from 1963 to 1979) was more eager to push ahead with the promotion of ethnic national culture in the 1970s, when his more authoritarian rule was reaching its apex. Thus, the regimes' successful construction of national identity and its representations implies that South Korean society had historical backgrounds favourable for the project, and that the regimes were competent in utilising those advantages, successfully persuading people into believing in their nationhood.

On the other hand, it is noteworthy that the formation of national identity was also affected by an external factor, which was the world order, presided over by the US during the Cold War. As Smith (1971, pp. 2–3) pointed out as early as 1971:

> The nation-state is the almost undisputed foundation of world order, the main object of individual loyalties, the chief definer of a man's identity. It is far more significant for the individual and for world security than any previous type of political and social organisation.

It could be argued that the implication of Smith's remark is that the formation of nation would be influenced by the world order, and that in this regard the internal construction of a nation's identity would also be influenced by the world order. However, this external factor in the formation of the modern nation-state and national identity does not seem to have attracted enough attention from those researchers who have inquired into theories of nations and nationalism. This is mainly because they tend only to focus on internal processes and factors of the formation of nation-states.

The South Korean government promoted itself with two large-scale overseas touring exhibitions over a long period, from 1957 to 1985, in the US, Western European countries and Japan (Chung, 2005, pp. 7–41; Hahn, 2012, pp. 138–70; Jang, 2015, pp. 167–97; Jang, 2016, pp. 456–71; Lin, 2016, pp. 383–400). These countries were major powers under the US-led world order – especially the US, which played a decisive role in the formation of the South Korean modern nation-state. For its own political ambition, the US encouraged South Korea to build its national identity on the basis of Korean culture and history. The South Korean government considered these exhibitions to be an important opportunity to prove its cultural sovereignty and legitimacy as an independent nation. The US government, intent on constructing the US-led world order and securing an ally in the Far East, was very much willing to give its approvals to Korean culture to be independent, unique and creative. Given its indifference to Korean culture before it took part in the Second World War, the US's drastic change of perspective on Korean culture shows that its interest reflected a new political meaning with regard to the Korean peninsula (Jang, 2016, pp. 464–6).

Nation, nationalism and national identity

After Great Han [Korea] Empire (1897–1910) lost her diplomatic rights to the Japanese empire in 1905, an East Asian term translated from "nation," *minjok* got more popular through Korean newspapers (Park, 2010, p. 70). At the same time, the discovery of *minjok* was followed by the rise of *minjokjuui* (ethnic nationalism). Likewise, both *minjok* and *minjokjuui* began to grow to be the most powerful words in their political and cultural influence. In his book on the "genealogy" of Korean nationalism, Shin defines nationalism in Korea as ethnic nationalism and translates *minjokjuui* as "ethnic nationalism," saying that he uses the term because it "involves emphases on descent and race, that is, on biology" (Shin, 2006, p. 223). As Eckert (1990a, p. 368) points out, "One of Korea's most striking characteristics has been its long and continuous existence as a unified country between 668 and 1910."

This may mean that Korea is the right place for the notion of ethnic nation to thrive. However, nationalism as a collective identity arguably arose when Korea encountered unprecedented threats from the outside world after opening her ports in 1876. As Shin argues, "in Korea nationalism arose primarily as a response to imperialism." He goes on to say that "enhancement of collective consciousness and internal solidarity among Koreans against the external threat was even more urgent. As a result, an organic notion of nation (that is, nation as immortal and indivisible) developed" (Shin, 2006, p. 229). In the same context, Eckert (1990b, pp. 406–7) argues that "Korea's occupation by Japan intensified nationalist sentiment to an unprecedented degree. And inequities and brutalities during the occupation also further inflamed Korean nationalism."

As scholars point out, it is noticeable that ethnic nationalism in Korea during Japanese colonial rule focused mainly on cultural aspects, characterised as cultural nationalism. Actually, it was almost the only alternative that

Koreans could choose, as they almost lost all means of military or political resistance to Japanese imperialism. In the limited space available to them under Japanese surveillance, Korean academics attempted to find and prove their subjectivity and national identity through studies of language, history and folklore (Robinson, 1988, pp. 83–126). Their efforts show that "nationalism uses the pre-existing, historically inherited proliferation of cultures or cultural wealth," as Gellner (1983[2006], p. 54) argues. Smith (1991, p. vii) also suggests that nations and nationalism should be understood not only "as an ideology or form of politics," but "as cultural phenomena as well." He adds that "nationalism, the ideology and movement must be closely related to national identity, a multidimensional concept, and extended to include a specific language, sentiments and symbolism."[5]

Interestingly, early pioneers of cultural nationalism in Korea were eager to find symbolic images of the nation, such as the national soul and a national progenitor, Dangun (Em, 2013, pp. 79–82).[6] Especial emphasis on Dangun even developed as a religion one year before Korea's colonisation by the Japanese empire. However, it cannot be said that Koreans secured a firm foundation for discovering and translating their material culture for themselves during the colonial era, even though Shin argues that "the new Korean intelligentsia had nurtured the process of grafting symbols of the modern nation-state onto the existing ethnic and cultural identity and developed Korean nationalism as a political force" (Shin, 2006, p. 229). This situation may explain how the Japanese monopoly of discovering and interpreting Korean material culture discouraged Koreans from paying attention to the field of material culture, even though a few Korean scholars in Korea and abroad began to research art history and archaeology as a modern discipline.

Ethnic national culture, the museum and representation

It was after liberation in 1945 that Koreans got to participate in the discovery and interpretation of their material culture through the national museum. NMK was established right after the liberation by the US military government in Korea (1945–1948). NMK launched its activities for discovering ethnic national culture following on from the museological legacy of the Government-General Museum. However, political disorder in the late 1940s and during the Korean War (1950–1953) hindered NMK and South Korean academics from making meaningful progress in their research on material culture. Although NMK attempted to lay the foundation of independent discovery and the interpretation of material culture for building the new Korean modern nation-state, the South Korean government's interest in the national museum was very limited.

Park Chung Hee's regime (1961–1979) began to pay fully fledged interest in the political potential of material culture. Park's regime propelled ethnic nationalism through the medium of the discourse of ethnic national culture, which could instantly arouse the basic emotion of community spirit in South Korean society (Oh, 1998, p. 123). As Eckert (1999, pp. 369–70) argues, "nationalism was preached by the state authorities as an ultimate civic virtue for which no sacrifice was too much," and "nationalism and Cold War ideologies have severely constrained intellectual life in both Koreas during the past half-century." This discourse of ethnic national culture was one of the most important legacies of national history.

Lee (2002, p. 54) contends that the museum policy of the Third Republic (1963–1972), under the name of modernisation of the fatherland, was to secure the legitimacy of the regime and to unite the the independent country under an umbrella of cultural sameness. This means that NMK began to be considered as a major cultural institution that could produce the discourse of ethnic national culture. He also adds that these plans were related to the securement of discrimination from colonial remnants and of the unique characteristic of Korean culture as an independent country in a globalised world (Lee, 2002, p. 55). In this regard, a close look at the relation between historiography and art history or archaeology in this period is also important for understanding the nationalist narrative of NMK. Jeon (1998, p. 180) has tried to trace the development of Park Chung Hee's cultural heritage policies. Jeon argues that the Park regime strengthened its cultural policy in accord with his emphasis on the discourse on nationalism. He also adds that Park's cultural policies were intended to show the populace his historical legitimacy and to disseminate the nationalist thinking that they should unite around Park.

Some researchers argue that the state-sponsored cultural policy in South Korea was influenced by the Japanese colonial cultural policy, pointing out their similarity in political orientation (Park, 2010, p. 67; Pai, 2001, p. 86). However, their arguments are only a part of the story. Although the South Korean government followed or adopted some of Japanese colonial cultural policies, it needs to be understood that its ultimate orientation was definitely leaning towards the formation of an independent nation-state and the establishment of national identity. It seems clear that the negative perspectives on Park's regime's cultural policy consequently discouraged researchers from examining to what extent NMK's nationalist narratives influenced the populace's recognition of Korean material culture, as well as their nationalist consciousness. A close look at the social education programmes conducted in NMK, especially from the 1970s onwards, may show NMK's role in the internalisation of the nationalist narrative towards material culture. In relation to these relevant works, this research explores why and how Korean material culture has been discovered, interpreted and narrated in the name of ethnic nationhood, especially in terms of practice by the national museum, which has not been thoroughly examined so far.

Scope of the research

This book aims to understand how NMK, as a national repository of material culture and the state's premier exhibition facility, has shaped and been shaped by Korean nationalism. This research explores the processes by which the National Museum in South Korea has discovered and interpreted material culture, using concepts of ethnic nationalism in the historical and political contexts of South Korean society, and attempts to understand how this nationalist interpretation has regulated the South Koreans' understanding of their material culture. In this context, this book investigates the historical process and context in which ethnic nationalism became a dominant discourse in South Korea, a discourse which established itself in national cultural institutes like NMK, and which resulted in the injection of ethnic nationalism into material culture.

Major contexts considered for this research are as follows. First, in terms of historical context, Korea's traditional perception of China and Japan and the drastic change in this perception in the 20th century are considered. This includes changes in cultural and political relations with China in terms of Korea's identity, as well as Japanese colonial rule, cultural imperialism and its legacy. The notion of a millennium-long unified Korean dynasty has also been an important issue in building the national identity of South Korea. Second, the political context includes the division of Korea into north and south since 1945, the Korean War between 1950 and 1953 and the nation building since liberation in 1945, and several domestic political upheavals such as military coups in 1961 and in 1979. Third, the diplomatic context includes issues such as the securement of the cultural sovereignty of South Korea as a pro-American country under the Cold War order, and the South Korean government's overseas Korean culture exhibitions project for cultural diplomacy.

This book consists of four chapters and ends with a conclusion. Chapter 1, "Japanese cultural imperialism, museums and Koreans," explores how Koreans began to see their material culture through the modern institution of the museum. In order to understand the development of the national museum in Korea, this chapter tries to understand the geopolitics of this part of the world at the end of the 19th century, and to understand how and why museums and exhibitions became forms of national expression in Korea. In this regard, the main focus is placed on the Imperial Household Museum (downgraded to and renamed as the Yi Royal Household Museum after the annexation of Korea by Japan in 1910), the first museum in Korea, which was established under the influence of the Japanese Residency-General in 1908, and the Government-General Museum (1915–1945).

Chapter 2, "Independence, the National Museum and the US," traces how NMK tried to develop an independent capability, and how it tried to define its mission and vision through interactions with the US Army Military Government in Korea and the Republic of Korea government (established in 1948). Of particular interest are American attempts to introduce new social, cultural and political standards to the civilisation of South Korea after the Second World War. This chapter also examines a series of experiences of South Korea in acquiring cultural citizenship on the world stage through overseas exhibitions, by which NMK tried to define the cultural identity of Korea, display it and internalise it.

Chapter 3, "Ethnic nationalism and museum narrative," focuses on the ethnic nationalist policy of Park Chung Hee's regime in terms of utilisation of the material culture through NMK. This regime took a fully fledged interest in the potential of material culture. Park pushed forward ethnic awareness as a means to mobilise the Korean people for the so-called modernisation of the fatherland. In this context, this chapter considers the ways in which he utilised Korean material culture for the solidarity of the people, and how he secured support for his political ambitions. This chapter also explores how Korean national identity was externally consolidated through material culture by overseas exhibitions from 1976 to 1985, and how this national identity was meant to be recognised by and instilled into South Koreans through NMK's activities, such as the renovation project, during this period.

Chapter 4, "National narrative and South Korean society," examines how the South Korean government tried to construct the increasingly essentialised and controlled communication of the national narrative towards South Korean society since the 1970s, focusing on the activities of NMK, which is considered to have played a major role in this process. This chapter also shows South Koreans' internalisation of the nationalist narrative during the 1980s and 1990s, discussing NMK's activities directed towards audiences and a series of reopening projects it undertook and their impacts on South Korean society.

Notes

1 'President Roh's address at NMK on 28 October 2005.' Available at: http://pa.go.kr/research/contents/speech/index.jsp. Accessed 16 January 2019.

2 Kim argues that cultural nationalism, a powerful driving force in the colonial and post-colonial eras, helped East Asian national museums join in nation building or nation-rebuilding and consolidate national identity. See Kim Hongnam, "Do Museums Matter?: Looking beyond Cultural Nationalism in Asia," unpublished

lecture, Victoria & Albert Museum, 7 July 2010. Available at: http://vimeo.com/22230347. Accessed 16 January 2019.

3 Knell (2011, p. 13) argues that NMK is saying "'this is us', 'we are not you', 'respect us and recognise us.'"

4 Lim (2004, p. 29) argues that the "dissolution of the discourse of national history means breaking up hegemonies on which to represent all the population's unitary intention and interest in the name of a nation and by doing so conceal and suppress differences within each individual nation."

5 In this regard, it is remarkable that an indigenous alphabet for the Korean people was invented and promulgated as early as 1446, and that it was utilised for publishing.

6 Dangun is one of the representative inventions of tradition, as per in Hobsbawm's argument (Hobsbawm, 1983, p. 7). Lee (2006, pp. 13–18) argues that modern Korean historiography, with no evidence to speak of, invented Dangun as a forefather of the nation.

1 Japanese cultural imperialism, museums and Koreans

The Korean encounter with exhibition and museum

The Kingdom of Joseon (1392–1897) was forced to open up in response to the gunboat diplomacy of the Japanese empire in 1876. The two countries signed the treaty of amity. As Cumings (2005, p. 102) argues, however, although "concluded in the name of sovereign equality and against the putative hierarchy of the Chinese order, the real effect of the treaty was to erase the centuries of essential equality between Japan and Korea." From this point on, this kingdom began to encounter modern Western institutions such as exhibitions and museums. It was in this context that Kim Gi-su (1832–?), who was sent as an envoy to Japan right after the opening of the kingdom, visited a Japanese museum in 1876.[1]

In 1881, Park Jeong-yang (1841–1905), who was a member of the Korean delegation to Japan, reported on modern institutions such as museums, saying, "the Bureau of Museums under the Ministry of Agriculture and Commerce administers affairs related to museums and extends knowledge by collecting natural and man-made, and past and present, objects."[2] The awareness of museums and the desire to see them established in Korea was, however, limited to a small reformist elite.

Gapsin jeongbyeon, a radical reformist coup that took place in 1884, failed in just three days, which gave another chance for Japan and China to intervene in the Korean government, and Korea now became the arena for competing political and economic interests in the region. At this time, unfavourable trade with Japan drove Korea's pre-modern economy into crisis (Lee, 1990, pp. 367–8). Nevertheless, the Korean government failed to reform its ineffective structure and to give up its dependence on world powers such as Japan and Russia. The 1894 Donghak uprisings, a nationwide movement of peasants designed to overthrow earlier feudal structures, which advocated against foreign intervention, ironically led to more foreign intervention, making Korea the battlefield between China and Japan. Japan, which had defeated China in the Sino-Japanese War of 1894–1895, now became the strongest power in East Asia, securing a firm base from which to colonise Korea. Gabo gyeongjang, a drastic governmental modernisation reform movement in 1894, was conducted under the influence of the empire of Japan, paving a smooth way for political and economic penetration of Korea by Japan (Lee, 1990, pp. 406–19).

In 1893, the Korean government participated in the World Columbian Exposition in Chicago. In 1895, the government directed the Ministry of Agriculture, Commerce and Industry to be responsible for exposition-related affairs. The Korean government also participated in the Exposition Universelle in Paris in 1900 (Kim, 2000, pp. 86–96). However, it appears that those participations had a diplomatic rather than commercial or industrial purpose. In 1897, the Joseon dynasty changed the country's name to the "Great Han Empire" in order to proclaim its full independence from China. Although the fledgling empire strove to make itself rich and strong, it did not have the leadership nor the capital to accomplish the task. A series of modern reforms in Korea could not help but be connected to intervention by foreign countries, which conveniently also was an excuse for those who were obsessed with feudalistic privilege to obstruct reforms for the contemporary mission of national prosperity and military power, civilisation and enlightenment.

This new empire, however, began to understand the importance of expositions and exhibitions in terms of the development of its industry and commerce. In 1902, it set up a temporary office for exposition-related affairs under the Ministry of Agriculture, Commerce and Industry, under the leadership of the minister.[3] In 1903, the Korean government participated in the fifth Japanese Domestic Exposition, and opened a display room for a temporary exhibition in Seoul on 1 June 1903.[4] In July 1904, the temporary office became a regular office called the Division of Industry Encouragement. The Museum for Encouraging Industry under the ministry was also mentioned in newspapers in 1906.[5] As can be seen, the Korean government aimed at achieving a modern standard of economic development, and understood expositions and museums in this context. The government, however, did not manage to accomplish this goal, and the museum itself could not draw attention from Korean society.

The government's efforts and tactics were not enough to maintain its independence against the Japanese intention of colonisation. The empire of Japan, which had beaten Russia in the Russo-Japanese War in 1904–1905, succeeded in depriving Korea of her diplomatic sovereignty by making Korea its protectorate in 1905 through successful negotiation with the US and the United Kingdom. In February 1906, the Japanese empire established the Residency-General, which paved the way for the colonisation of Korea. Therefore, exhibitions and museums could only draw attention in terms of securing foundations of economic development rather than of searching for or displaying national identity by exhibiting Korean culture to the public.

Establishment of the Imperial Household Museum and its colonial intention

In June 1907, Emperor Gojong (r. 1864–1907) sent his secret envoys to the Second Hague Peace Conference in order to appeal to the world powers about the unlawful intervention in Korea by the empire of Japan. However, the Korean envoys were never allowed to participate in this conference. In retribution, Japan forced Emperor Gojong to abdicate the throne and installed his son Sunjong (r. 1907–1910) in his place. In August 1907, Japan appointed a Japanese vice minister in every Korean government ministry, in order to accomplish a more systematic intervention in Korea's internal affairs. From November that year, all laws and regulations had to be screened by the Residency-General. Furthermore, the Korean army was disbanded on August 1907. It was during this period that the Ministry of the Imperial Household discussed the establishment of a museum under the ministry.

When Komiya Mihomatsu (1859–1935), a Japanese vice minister of the ministry, described the establishment of the Imperial Household Museum in the preface of the *Catalogue of Yi Royal Household Museum Collection*, he recorded that he conceived the establishment of the museum, zoo and garden for the sake of the new emperor.[6] However, the Residency-General was actually looking for solutions to quell public sentiment aggravated by its de facto seizure of power. One of the solutions was to show Koreans that Korea was developing as a modern nation thanks to Japan's help, as shown by the argument that the museum, zoo and botanical garden were developed as popular institutions emblemmatic of a new stage of Korea's civilisation (Park, 2004, p. 157; Park, 2009, p. 194). As Lee (2004, pp. 275–6) points out, the museum, zoo and botanical garden of the Imperial Household were considered by the Japanese colonial authorities to be one of the most important accomplishments of the Residency-General.

On 13 August 1908, the Ministry of the Imperial Household established the Bureau of the Royal Garden. According to the bureau's office, as of May 1909, the Division of Museums under the bureau was in charge of affairs relating to the collection, display and storage of historical artefacts, works of art, craftworks and natural products.[7] However, this museum soon described itself as a fine art museum. From January to August 1908, the museum collected 8,600 items, and in September 1908 these were all displayed in chronological order.[8] The museum was opened to the public on 1 November 1909; the Bureau of Royal Garden sent notices to public and private schools recommending that students visit. Koreans experienced modern institutions and encountered their material culture through this museum. Therefore, Koreans had to accept a new order of civilisation that Japanese colonialists were offering to them: that is, the Japanese intended to dominate Korea through colonial rule (Figure 1.1).

Following the annexation in 1910, the Government-General encouraged Korean local officials and elites to organise tourist parties and a tour around Seoul, allegedly a new centre civilised by colonial rule. These tourist parties visited modern institutions such as the museum and zoo, hospitals and industrial facilities and so forth. In the Japanese colonial context, this tour was not just simply for sightseeing; it was a ritual, an eye-opening introduction to a new civilisation. The Imperial Household Museum became just one component of this spectacle showing off the accomplishments and prospects of colonial rule.

Following Japan's defeat of Qing's China in the Sino-Japanese war in 1894, the Japanese elite became increasingly interested in the Korean peninsula. As debates on the conquest of Korea started in earnest in Japanese politics, this elite needed to broaden its knowledge of Korea as a target of colonisation. The Japanese government pushed forward its so-called "investigation of old customs" of Korea, which included Korean material culture (Park, 1998, pp. 62–72). In 1902, Tokyo Imperial University

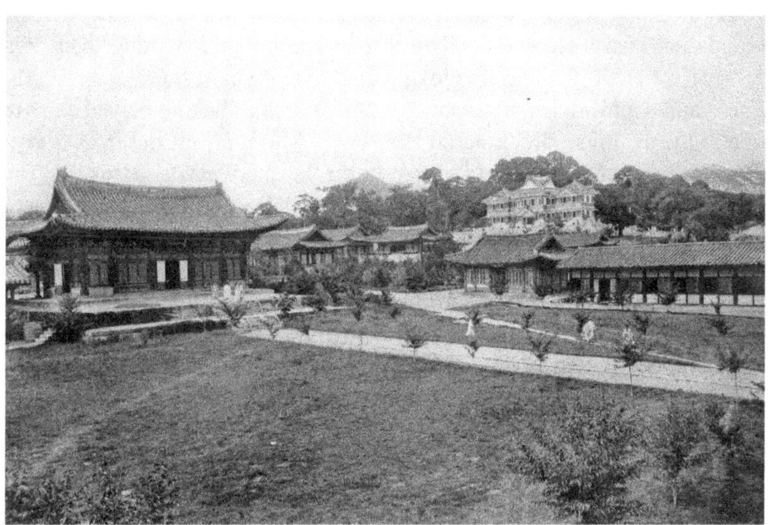

Figure 1.1 The Yi Royal Household Museum. Reprinted from *Liōke hakubutsukan shojōhin shasinchō* [Catalogue of the Yi Royal Household Museum Collection], Seoul: Yi Royal Household Museum, 1912.

gave Sekino Tadashi (1868–1935) the task of surveying Korean traditional architecture, as well as ancient tombs, ceramics and Buddhist statues. His report played a major role in constructing the Japanese discourse on Korean material culture.[9] In 1909, at the Korean government's request, he surveyed Korean architecture with his assistants, Yatsui Seiichi (1880–1959) and Kuriyama Shunichi (1882–?), who would later become specialists in Korean material culture of the colonial period (Pai, 2013, pp. 116–18).

Sekino, a historian of Japanese architecture, was the first scholar to survey Korean material culture using modern research methods. It seems that he had been preoccupied with the political situation when Korea was considered an uncivilised nation. He paid much attention to the accomplishments of ancient Korea, such as the Buddhist culture of the Three Kingdoms Period (traditionally 57 BCE–668 CE) and the Unified Silla Period (676–935), and celadon of the Goryeo dynasty (918–1392). However, the culture of the Joseon dynasty (1392–1910), which he thought had so many evils, could not be justly evaluated because of his pre-established view. He believed that the Joseon dynasty was a period of decline and decadence in art and craft techniques, particularly in the latter years (Sekino, 1910, p. 43). In this colonial view, the decline of the dynasty was directly related to the decline of its culture, justifying Japan's political and academic intervention in Korea. His argument concerning the decline of the culture of the Joseon dynasty was not widely debated and therefore became a firmly established theory.[10]

Likewise, it was these Japanese scholars who began to construct the foundation of a discourse on Korean material culture, creating their own perspective on the general stream of Korean traditional culture in the 1900s. The opinion and advice of Japanese scholars such as Sekino played a major role in the exhibits. The Imperial Household Museum was not in any position to construct its own perspective in the Japanese academic world. The vice minister of the Office of the Yi Royal Household, Komiya, also mentioned in the 1912 catalogue that:

> what the Yi Royal Household Private Museum has done is just to collect once dispersed diverse artefacts in one place. We cannot help postponing a systematic research on Korean art and crafts. This catalogue is just for providing scholars with resources for research as well as for meeting antiquarians' needs.
>
> (Yi Royal Household Museum, 1912, pp. 3–7)

This meant that those who were in charge of that museum did not consider it their mission to conduct a fully-fledged research on Korean material culture. This was proved by the fact that this museum never employed any professional scholars until colonial rule ended in 1945 (Jang, 2015, pp. 32–3).

The Korean encounter with "national" material culture

In the pre-modern era, the Korean elites, who had considered it their ultimate goal in their private and political life to achieve virtuous ideals centred on a neo-Confucianist perspective of the world, were not familiar with the new epistemological category of material culture. Paintings and calligraphy had been respected as a means of cultivating the minds of the literati class, but architecture, sculpture and craft works were not considered as anything more than practical skills or techniques for daily life.[11] It was not until the encounter with the Japanese and Western powers that Koreans began to recognise that those fields could be categorised as important to the "national material culture."[12]

Beginning with the opening of Korean ports to Japan in 1876, the Japanese and foreigners who came to Korea began to demand exotic "Korean" cultural objects, such as celadon masterpieces which were stolen from tombs in the Gaeseong area, the former capital of the Goryeo dynasty. Some Japanese immigrants and merchants realised that the trade in celadon paid well, and they began to take the lead in grave robberies.[13] The Korean government, at a low point, could hardly eradicate grave robberies. Antique shops managed by the Japanese began to emerge from 1895 and thrived in Seoul in the 1900s (Kwon, 2008, pp. 205–11). Korean material culture therefore became known at home and abroad from the late 19th century on (Horlyck, 2013, pp. 475–9).

With the Japanese taking the lead in grave robbery and the trading of celadon and other old objects, Koreans began to recognise the value of these things from a new perspective. These old objects were simply considered to be rare and peculiar objects at first; later, their cash value became known. The objects were also expected to act as a stimulus to revive Korea's underdeveloped industry. More importantly, they began to be considered as national treasures that the Japanese were stealing, in much the same way that Japanese colonialism was intervening in Korean politics. This is the point at which material culture came to have national implications, and the category of old fine arts started to have political and national meaning in Korea.

In April 1910, four months before the annexation, *Daehan maeil sinbo* published an article titled "If Treasures of the Country Disappear."[14] At most 30 years ago, Koreans had hardly thought that "old objects concealed in golden boxes and stone chambers as well as treasures buried countryside" would be national treasures with which to "preserve the glory of the country and cultivate country's spirit". Although there were not many Korean intellectuals, some began to give the name of their nation to their material culture, considering the transfer of cultural objects to Japan in the same context as the idea that the Japanese intended to usurp the national sovereignty of Korea. In this regard, national pride in cultural objects was expected to provide Koreans with a basis of hope for the nation's prosperity and independence.[15]

Furthermore, Korean elites began to worry about the Japanese hegemony over the discovery and interpretation of Korean material culture. *Hwangseong shinmun* reported a contribution on Sekino's lecture, lamenting that Japanese scholars were monopolising the discovery and interpretation of Korean material culture.[16] However, he could not make an adequate counter-argument against Sekino's argument. His frustration deepened, because the semi-colonial status of Korea was also considered to be clear evidence supporting Sekino's argument. In this way, Japanese discourse on material culture began to carry weight, and Koreans were inevitably influenced by the Japanese perspective.

Within three months of the annexation in August 1910, colonial authorities forced all of the Korean nationalist newspapers to cease publishing, and Japanese oppressive colonial rule was enforced throughout the new colony by military police. No more nationalist interpretations of Korean material culture would be reported in the press. Notably, classes on Korean history were also abolished at public primary schools one year after the annexation, and this policy ultimately forced private schools to give up such classes up until September 1913 (Jang, 2004, pp. 12–16). From this point on, national history under colonial rule meant *Japanese* national history.

Under this situation, the Government-General organ, *Maeil sinbo* [the Daily News] repeatedly reported Sekino's accomplishments, saying that "Dr. Sekino discovered two wooden buildings of the Goryeo dynasty. This is a great discovery in the history of Korean Architecture."[17] Sekino, who was described as a figure of authority with a background of modern learning, was depicted to be a discoverer of Korean material culture as well. The official press also reported that Korean historical remains were preserved only by virtue of colonial rule. For example, the first governor-general, Terauchi Masatake (in office from 1910 to 1916), championed conservation projects such as the Seokguram grotto in Gyeongju, an 8th-century cave temple with a magnificent stone Buddha statue (Gang, 2012, p. 97; Pai, 2013, pp. 128–30). In short, Japanese colonialists were eager to position themselves as discoverers and interpreters of Korean material culture. It was in this context that the Government-General Museum was established five years after the annexation.

The Government-General Museum and the Japanese colonial view of Korean history

The Government-General Museum (GGM) was established at Gyeongbokgung Palace in Seoul on 1 December 1915. The only permanent building built for the Products Exhibition of 1915 for commemorating the fifth year of colonial rule was converted into the GGM (Kal, 2011, pp. 16–22; Jang, 2015, pp. 38–40). The colonial authorities needed an official museum to represent the material culture of Korea under the name of the Government-General, although Yi Royal Household Museum (hereafter YHM) was under their control. From a colonial perspective, GGM was to be the only museum to have official status as a museum that represented the identity of Korea (Figure 1.2).

Furthermore, Governor-General Terauchi was very much interested in the utilisation of museum projects and the investigation of historic remains (Fujita, 1953, pp. 67–88). He entrusted Sekino with launching research into the historical remains of Korea (Atkins, 2010, p. 111). The establishment of GGM in December 1915 preannounced a fully-fledged investigation of historic remains in Korea. GGM was expected to take charge of every affair related to the investigation of historic remains as well as the management of the museum. GGM's projects were intended to stabilise colonial rule as well as gain international recognition of Japan's position. These projects were seen as an effective way of getting Koreans to consent to colonial rule. The colonial authorities wanted Korean culture to be seen as part of Japanese – and, more generally, East Asian – culture, ensuring that Korean ethnic feelings would be suppressed.[18]

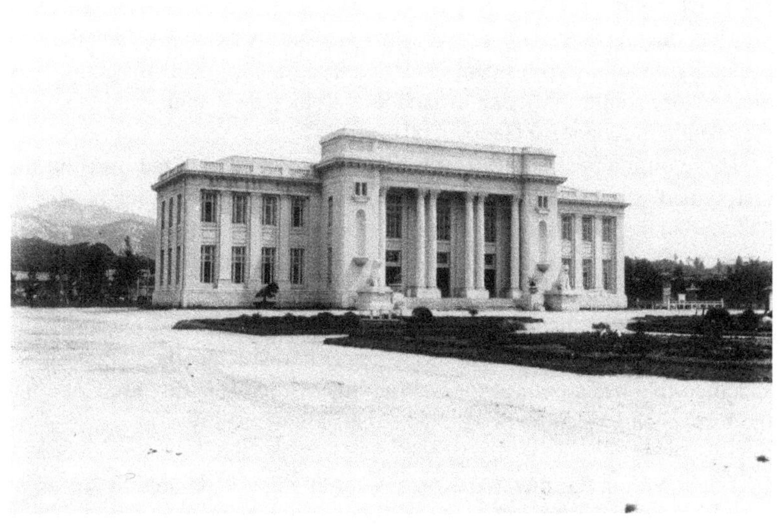

Figure 1.2 The Government-General Museum. With kind permission from NMK.

This is why Terauchi pushed forward with these projects as part of the assimilation policy. Colonial authorities' consideration of cultural fields was an alternative, "soft" way of controlling hegemony in the colonial society, although the oppressive colonial rule and suppression of the press were commonplace in the 1910s. The GGM projects and exhibitions were meant to find resources for constructing the logic of effective colonial rule in the history of Korea and East Asia and, by doing so, develop a new identity for Japan.

In this regard, the most important key word of colonial rule in Korea from the early stage was *assimilation* (Caprio, 2009, pp. 81–5; Henry, 2014, pp. 92–113). In July 1913, governor general Terauchi stated that the fastest way to assimilate people of the new territory into Japan was to train them through education.[19] Although the Government-General consistently emphasised the policy of assimilation, however, it realised that the task was never easy. An internal report forwarded to the governor-general written by a high-ranking Japanese official at the Government-General in October 1910 admitted that Koreans' national consciousness was the toughest obstacle to the policy.[20] This report also proposed that study of Koreans' mentality, history and national consciousness, rather than political policies, should be undertaken. It is evident that the colonial authorities had difficulty in dealing with Korean "national" consciousness, which began to thrive after the opening of the country and the imperial intervention of world powers. Furthermore, Korean nationalist intellectuals convincingly argued that the Korean nation had been one nation since Dangun had built the country, emphasising shared, collective memories. Mojichi Rokusaburo, a colonial bureaucrat, a former high-ranking Japanese official who had worked in the 1910s, recalled the difficulties that the Government-General faced, saying, "Koreans don't think their culture is inferior to that of Japanese. Rather, they think that in the past they taught the Japanese (Jeong, 2001, p. 87)."[21]

These difficulties reaffirmed the necessity of studying and utilising the history and culture of the colony. The basic logic of assimilation needed to be found in them by Japanese scholars, which was one of the most important demands from the colonial officials. It is in this context that in July 1916 colonial authorities launched the compilation of *Chosen hantoshi* [History of the Korean Peninsula]. The purpose of this project was to "notify the mercy of annexation to assimilate Koreans psychologically." This project specified two basic criteria for writing this history: one, to "establish that the Korean and Japanese people were one nation"; and two, to:

> elaborate on the fact that Koreans could enjoy happiness by virtue of the prosperous age at last, even though Koreans had become poor and weak experiencing the rise and fall of the heroes and dynastic revolutions from ancient times to the Joseon dynasty.[22]

As shown in Terauchi's remark in July 1913, the colonial authorities argued from the beginning of colonial rule that both the Korean and Japanese nations had the same ancestry; they persisted in this view throughout colonial rule. Their argument was also accompanied by another belief: that is, in the incompetency and decline of the Korean nation. Therefore, annexation and colonial rule could be explained and justified in this way: civilised relatives (Japanese) helped the uncivilised relatives (Koreans) who could never enlighten themselves (Atkins, 2010, pp. 56–7). As Lee (1990, pp. 1–3) points out, scholars in Japanese official academic circles created this colonial view of history and tried to instil it in Koreans, presenting the heteronomy, stagnation and factionalism of Korean society as their evidence.

They argued that Korea, which is located on a peninsula, is inevitably "other-directed," and that this is why Korea had served China. The argument went as follows: this heteronomy resulted in stagnation and Korea's characteristic factionalism, which can easily be found in the political history of the Joseon dynasty, worsened the stagnation, bringing about its ultimate decline.[23] They considered it their mission to evidence their arguments and persuade Koreans into believing them. In particular, they made efforts to prove the importance of the influence of Chinese civilisation on Korea in the fields of archaeology and art history. From the beginning, their conclusion was that Korea had been dependent on Chinese culture, and therefore Korean culture had stagnated, especially during the Joseon period.[24]

In this regard, the Japanese scholars put efforts into researching a Chinese commandery, Nangnang (Lolang in Chinese), which had been located in a north-western part of the Korean peninsula. The culture of this commandery, which was established in 108 BCE and existed until 313 CE, was offered as firm evidence to prove Korea's heteronomy to Chinese culture. Japanese archaeologists at GGM excavated many tombs from this period but misunderstood them, thinking that they had found a culture typical of China proper (Oh, 2006, pp. 15–27). Their assumption was that this culture had brought civilisation to the Korean peninsula. This became a fixed theory, suggesting that no civilisation had existed before the influx of the Chinese culture into Korea. Their arguments bolstered the preconception that Korea should not have its own independent prehistoric culture.

The culture of the Silla dynasty from the Three Kingdoms drew special attention, because the remains uncovered showed astonishing accomplishments such as splendid golden crowns and accessories. Archaeological achievements found in Gyeongju, which was the capital of the Silla dynasty, contributed to boosting the authority of Japanese scholars as discoverers and interpreters of Korean culture. Their authority also contributed to giving credibility to their unproven arguments, such as the supposed conquest of Silla by Empress Jingū (ca. 169–269 CE) and the colonisation of Gaya, one of the ancient polities, located between Silla and Baekje, by ancient Japan between the mid-4th and mid-6th centuries.[25]

Likewise, archaeological investigations were actively utilised to prove the colonial view of history, and GGM was at the centre of this discovery. GGM utilised human resources from the Japanese academic world. Most researchers were graduates from Tokyo Imperial University or Kyoto Imperial University. GGM pushed forward with a series of excavation projects throughout Korea in order to fulfil its academic interests and ambitions. It was by the hands of these Japanese academics that GGM published the 15 volumes of the *Catalogue of Historical Remains of Korea* between 1915 and 1935, the 16 volumes of the *Report of the Research of Antiquities* between 1917 and 1937, the 7 volumes of the *Special Report of the Research of Antiquities* from 1919 to 1930, the 2 volumes of the *Catalogue of Historical Remains and Treasures of Korea* from 1938 to 1940, and the 17 volumes of the *Museum Exhibits Illustrated* between 1926 and 1943 (Kim, 2009, pp. 126–7; Atkins, 2010, pp. 111–13).

This approach to the Korean material culture by these Japanese researchers was connected to a general trend in the Japanese academic world. The Japanese scholars wanted to construct their own perspectives on both Korean and Chinese cultures for understanding the Japanese culture. The relationship between Korea and Japan was also important in the same context. An official document written in 1925 explained that GGM's achievements "made it possible to study the origin of Japanese art, of which artists all over the world were full of admiration now."[26]

Koreans' response to the Japanese monopoly of the discourse on Korean material culture

To oppose Japanese scholars' control of the discourse on Korean culture, most Korean scholars focused on Korean history and language, as they believed that they had a competitive advantage over the Japanese. Beginning in the 1890s, Korean historians made efforts to prove the historical existence of Dangun (Lee, 2007, pp. 64–70). Dangun was considered by Korean historians and journalists to be on the grounds on which the Korean ethnic nation should maintain its independence.[27] It seems that, in competing with the Japanese, instilling a nationalist consciousness through historical studies was considered to be more effective than studying material culture, where a modern way of research and academic background was needed.

Furthermore, Koreans, who were surprised by, and ashamed of, the fact that it was Japanese that had discovered and interpreted Korean material culture on Koreans' behalf, soon began to realise that those monuments were their own cultural heritage. The accomplishments derived from the investigation and excavation projects by GGM contributed to disseminating a nationalist implication of the cultural objects. The three golden crowns excavated in the 1920s from royal tombs of Silla dynasty were important representative cultural objects of the Korean ethnic nation due to their uniqueness and beauty.[28] It was clear that the Japanese authorities secured their status as discoverers of Korean material culture, but cultural objects excavated in Korea also came to have the potential to stimulate Koreans' nationalist sentiments.

Nationwide touring lectures on Silla's cultural remains, which were organised for collecting donations by two private schools, Gyenam School and Nammyeong School in the Gyeongju area, were a good example showing this possibility. Korean newspapers contributed to furthering this nationalist pride in Koreans by reporting on these lectures.[29] The lecture tours took place from 1923 to 1926 and visited almost every big city in Korea, including Seoul, Daejeon, Pyongyang and Incheon, as well as some smaller counties. An editorial in *The Dong-A Ilbo* stated, "If we, Korea, did not have Gyeongju, how could we prove and say indigenous culture?" The cultural remains of Gyeongju were emerging as pride of Koreans.[30] When a robbery at the Gyeongju branch museum of GGM took place in 1927, the stolen cultural objects were described as "national treasures" even in the official newspaper of the Government-General.[31]

If the monuments and artefacts were believed to be not properly preserved by the colonial authorities, nationalistic anger among Koreans was aroused. Nationalist newspapers fiercely criticised the requirements needed for the preservation of cultural remains. The main point of their criticism was the colonial administration that fell behind its own standard. They emphasised their argument that the poor preservation of remains and discrimination in their preservation were effective ways to attack the policy foundation of assimilation of the colonial authorities. Interestingly, they focused their criticism on the improper preservation of Dangun-related remains, and fiercely called on the colonial authorities to account for the neglect of those remains.

In December 1926, a renowned writer, Choi Nam-seon (1890–1957), contributed an article, "Key Factor of the Preservation of Historical Remains," to *The Dong-A Ilbo*, focusing on the preservation of the Dangun remains.[32] He argued that their investigation and preservation never focused on the remains which Koreans had cherished. A newspaper article titled "A Shameful Stigma, the Nangnang Excavation Team" also pointed out that Koreans were unable to confront Japanese scholars, arguing that Koreans had had their history stolen because the Japanese had monopolised the discovery and interpretation of Korean material culture.[33] Although Korean nationalist historians strove to compile Korean history by emphasising the role of Dangun, it was actually not possible to contradict the Japanese interpretation of Nangnang culture through archaeological investigations. Criticism by Korean journalists resulted in doubts about the academic truthfulness of the Japanese investigation. What they were keen to secure was the discovery and interpretation of Korean relics by Koreans.

However, Korean intellectuals never did have the competitiveness that the Japanese had. Only a few Koreans started their careers as art historians or researchers on prehistory either in Korea or abroad in the 1930s. Even Korean intellectuals internalised the discourse by the Japanese on Korean material culture. Furthermore, it was extremely difficult for Korean researchers to enter the Japanese academic world. In this context, those challenges did not evolve into fully-fledged and persistent interests and professional researches.

Colonial policy on museums and cultural objects during the war period

Ever since the empire of Japan invaded Manchuria to the north of Korea in September 1931, the empire, including its colony, Korea, was reorganised on a war footing. This political situation gradually gave this colony an importance as a logistics base of human and material resources. In 1935, the colonial authorities launched the so-called Simjeon (literally "a field of heart") Cultivation Movement, a public campaign to give people spiritual and practical norms on a war footing. This official campaign was intended to cultivate subjects loyal to the interests of the Japanese empire and emperor, and to attract a more effective mobilisation for the war. On 20 June 1935, *Mail sinbo* published "Opening Service of the Museum as a Side Operation of Simjeon Cultivation Movement," which showed their intention to politically utilise the museum and cultural objects.

The Museum Week, which had begun in November 1933, also shows that these actions taken by the colonial authorities were for the purpose of persuading people to recognise cultural objects and historical remains as a communal ground for the national solidarity of the empire. The Government-General established 10 September 1935 as the Penchant Day for Historical Remains. This was another attempt to utilise cultural heritage for national unity. These government-sponsored events included radio broadcasting, distribution of posters at central government level, lectures and talks by private organisations, the prevention campaign against tomb robbery and instructions for students at a local level. Ultimately, all of these actions were intended to appease the Korean people and instil in them the notion that Japan and Korea were one ethnic nation.

However, colonial authorities did not forget to utilise YHM in terms of the promotion of the notion. The existence of the Yi Royal Household and its collaboration with the authorities was an effective means to justify policies executed by the colonial authorities. In 1933, YHM launched permanent exhibitions of Japanese "modern" fine arts at Seokjojeon Hall (a Western-style building) in Deoksugung Palace.[34] YHM, not GGM, began to display Japanese art under the name of the Yi Royal household. The colonial authorities wanted to display an image of harmony and mutual understanding. They hoped that the Yi Royal household would function as a symbol of the notion that Japan and Korea were one ethnic nation. In 1938, YHM launched a permanent exhibition of ancient Korean art at a newly built Western-style building right next to Seokjojeon Hall. What was intended was harmony between Korean and Japanese art, the Korean and Japanese ethnic nations, old and new. However, the reality was that the museum had to change its name to the Yi Royal Household Museum of Art in order not to be seen to challenge the authority of GGM.[35]

The political intention of the cultural heritage policies became conspicuous with the outbreak of the Sino-Japanese war in July 1937. *The Dong-A Ilbo* reported that the Penchant Day for Historical Remains was meant to put emphasis on the preservation of these remains, and the undeniable fact that Japan and Korea were one nation.[36] On 10 September 1937, Shiobara Tokisaburo, the Japanese director of the Bureau of Education at the Government-General, said in his radio address commemorating the Penchant Day for Historical Remains:

> This campaign should not end in only the preservation of materialistic remains. These historical remains prove the notion that Korea and Japan are one nation. By realising and cherishing this notion, I think we should cultivate a faith as inhabitants of this peninsula, as well as loyal subjects of the empire of Japan.[37]

What the campaign really meant became clear in this totalitarian and militarist situation. From October 1937 on, colonial authorities began to disseminate a slogan called "Pledge of Imperial Subjects," the first sentence of which was, "We should repay the emperor's country with loyalty as we are subjects of the empire." Furthermore, an all-out national mobilisation movement commenced from July 1938 throughout Korea.

It is interesting to note that Korean people visiting GGM drastically increased from 1937 (see Table 1.1). From 1924 to 1936, the percentage of Japanese visitors vis-à-vis total visitors was higher than that of Korean visitors for all but three years. This implies that Koreans were not the main audience of GGM. The drastic increase in the Korean audience from 1937 seems

Table 1.1 Visitors to GGM, 1924 to 1940

Year	*GGM (Seoul)*			
	Total	*Korean*	*Japanese*	*Foreigner*
1924	60,309	19,750	38,784	1,775
1925	49,061	27,483	21,182	996
1926	60,125	32,471	25,648	2,006
1927	44,716	15,280	28,129	1,307
1928	50,388	18,859	30,308	1,221
1929	46,639	16,349	28,935	1,355
1930	36,604	9,304	25,787	1,513
1931	36,142	13,980	20,763	1,399
1932	49,742	11,131	37,966	645
1933	41,371	14,577	26,099	695
1934	49,465	19,342	28,523	1,600
1935	57,165	28,004	27,526	1,635
1936	63,111	28,829	32,392	1,890
1937	98,687	61,986	34,772	1,929
1938	85,865	50,875	34,140	850
1939	104,322	62,954	39,014	2,354
1940	145,392	104,148	39,607	1,637

Source: Compiled from the Government-General of Korea, *Chōsen sōtokubu shisei nenpō* [Annual Reports of the Government-General of Korea], 1926 to 1942, and Government-General of Korea, *Chōsen shakai kyōiku yōran* [A General Survery of Social Education in Korea], 1941, pp. 83–4.

to have been because the colonial authorities mobilised Koreans to attend exhibitions of GGM, including a special exhibition in 1938 titled *Relations between Korea and Japan in the Ancient Period*, for the purpose of urging Korean people to accept the notion that Korea and Japan were one ethnic nation.[38] It could also be understood in the same context that YHM also saw a drastic increase in audiences from 1938 (NMK, 2009, pp. 285–99). These increases demonstrate that the colonial authorities attempted to utilise the cultural heritage of Korea for their political ambitions.

In this totalitarian and militarist situation, Korean newspapers could not report their criticism at all. Rather, they just reported that Koreans had not paid enough attention to their cultural heritage, and that the Government-General would reinforce punishment and survey their destruction. It was not possible to criticise the policies and intentions of the Government-General any more from the late 1930s.

Although it was not possible for Korean collectors to intervene in an official interpretation of Korean material culture, some had a clear nationalist motivation for collecting artefacts and cultural material. A Korean great landowner, Jeon Hyong-phil (1906–1962), started to collect Korean cultural objects from 1930 with the assistance of Korean specialists such as Oh Se-chang (1864–1953), who maintained the tradition from the Joseon dynasty as a calligrapher and collector (Kim, 2013, pp. 104–11). Jeon even established a private museum in Seoul in 1938, although it failed to open to the public before the liberation (Lee, 2011, pp. 128–9). Jeon's Korean paintings and ceramic collection as a private collection have been estimated as second to none in quality in South Korea. In addition to Jeon, there was a dozen famous Korean collectors, some of whom maintained their collections and donated them to NMK after liberation.[39]

There were only a few Korean scholars who studied Korean material culture. Go Yu-seop (1905–1944), who majored in aesthetics and art history at Keijo Imperial University, was almost the only researcher on Korean art history. In 1933, he became the director of the Gaeseong Municipal Museum, and, as the only Korean museum curatorial staff in Korea, dedicated himself to the research of Korean art history. He is argued to have built the modern foundation of Korean art history (Kim, 2002, pp. 507–18).[40] However, his limitations have also been pointed out; he was affected by Japanese scholars' views, for example, their low estimation of the culture of the Joseon dynasty (Kim, 2002, pp. 508–15). Other than art historians, there were some Korean folklorists and archaeologists, some of whom studied in European universities. However, it was not easy for them to get regular jobs in the field and confront Japanese scholars from their own perspectives, although they conducted their studies with nationalist motives.

Notes

1 Kim Gi-su, *Ildonggiyu* [Record of a Journey to Japan], 1877, cited in Cha Mun-seong, *Geundae bangmulgwan – geu hyeongseong gwa byeoncheon gwajeong* [Modern Museum: Its Formation and Transition], Paju: Korean Academic Information, 2008, pp. 154–61.

2 Park Jeong-yang, *Ilbonguk nongsangmuseong gakguk gyuchik* [Report on the Job Description of the Ministry of Agriculture and Commerce at the Japanese Government], 1881.

3 *Gojongsillok* [Annals of King Gojong], 12 July 1902, Imperial Order no.10: the establishment of the Temporary Office for Expositions; Ministerial Ordinance no.39: Regulation on the Temporary Office for Exposition.

4 "Mulpum jinyeol [Display of Products]," *Hwangseong shinmun*, 2 June 1903.

5 "Gwangmu 11 nyeondo chongyesan [Government Budget for the Year 1907]," *Hwangseong shinmun*, 26 December 1906.

6 The Yi Royal Household Museum, "Shogen [Preface]," *Liōke hakubutsukan shojōhin shasinchō* [Catalogue of the Yi Royal Household Museum Collection], Seoul: YHM, 1912. See Jang, 2015, pp. 22–29.

7 "Eowon samuguk bunjang gyujeong [Regulation on the Office of the Royal Garden]," 18 May 1909, Article 1.

8 When this museum published the catalogue of the collection in 1912, it boasted of its collection of 12,230 items, which comprised Buddha statues, metal works, stone works, wooden works, lacquer ware, embroidery, textiles, ceramics, roof tiles, glass works, paintings etc (YHM, 1912).

9 Sekino is considered the first modern historian of Korean art. His representative writings include *Kankoku kenchiku chōsa hōkoku* [Report on Investigation of Korean Architecture] (Tokyo: 1904), *Sina no kenchiku to geijutsu* [Architecture and Art of China] (Tokyo: Iwanami shoten, 1938), *Chōsen bijutsusi* [A History of Korean Art] (Seoul: Chosen sigakukai, 1932) and *Kankoku no kenchiku to geijutsu* [Architecture and Art of Korea] (Tokyo: Iwanami shoten, 1941).

10 Sekino concludes in his 1932 book that Korea did not have capability to maintain its independence from China and Japan, and that it had fallen into toadyism and the persistence of the old order, with its people losing their energy (Sekino, 1932, pp. 3–7).

11 See Clunas, 1997, p. 9. He argues that "Chinese art" is quite a recent invention. According to him, "although the textiles, pieces of calligraphy, paintings, sculptures, ceramics, and other works date from a period of 5,000 years, the idea of grouping this body of material together and calling it 'Chinese art' has a much shorter history."

12 Korea established diplomatic relations with the US in 1882, the UK and Germany in 1883, and Russia and Italy in 1884.

13 From 1897 to 1909, 33 cases relating to the robbery of cultural objects were reported. 27 of them were by Japanese immigrants. See Lee Sun-ja, *Iljegangjeomgi gojeokjosasaeop yeongu* [Investigation Projects of Historic Remains in the Japanese Colonial Period] (Seoul: Gyeonginmunhwasa, 2009), pp. 22–24.

14 Anon., "Nara ui bobae eobseojineun han [if Treasures of the Country Disappear]," *Daehan maeil sinbo*, 12 April 1910.

15 Anon., "Gomul jinyeolso eseo goryeojagi lul bogo gamtanhameul igiji motanora [I can't stop admiring Goryeo celadon]," *Daehan maeil sinbo*, 25 March 1910.

16 Anon., "Sisa pyeongnon [Editorial Comment]," *Hwangseong shinmun*, 26 November 1909.

17 Anon., "Joseon Choigo ui bomul [The Oldest Treasures of Korea]," *Maeil sinbo*, 1 January 1913.

18 See "Chōsen sōtokubu hakubutsukan oyobi koseki chōsa kaiyō [Outline of the Government-General Museum and Investigation Project of Historical Remains and Relics]," written by the Bureau of Education, the Government-General of Korea (April 1925). Available at: http://www.museum.go.kr/modern-history/doc.do?pseq=3400. Accessed 16 January 2019. See also Jang, 2015, p. 42.

19 "Sanae chongdok dam – gyoyuk bangchim [Talk with Governor General Terauchi: Educational Policy]," *Maeil sinbo*, 22 July 1913.

20 "Kyōka ikensho [A Written Opinion on Edification], 8 October 1910," cited in Lee Ji-won, *Hanguk geundae munhwa sasangsa yeongu* [The History of Korean Modern Cultural Thought], Seoul: Hyean, 2007, p. 92.

21 Mojichi Rokusaburo, "Chōsen tōchiron [Theory of Adminstration of Korea]," *Saito makoto bunsho* [Documents of Saito Makoto] (Tokyo: Komasholin, 1975), cited in Jeong Sang-woo, *Joseon chongdokbu ui joseonsa pyeonchan saeop* [Government-General of Korea's Compilation Project of History of Korea], unpublished PhD thesis, Seoul National University, 2011, p. 87.

22 Government-General of Korea, *Chōsen hantōshi hensei no yōsi oyobi junjyo* [Essentials and Sequences of Compilation of the History of the Korean Peninsula], 1916, pp. 1–5, cited in Jeong, 2001, p. 28.

23 *Chōsenshi no shirube* [A Guide to Korean History], compiled in 1936 by the Government-General of Korea, shows these perspectives on Korean history by Japanese historians.

24 Sekino is a representative Japanese scholar who stuck to these arguments. See Sekino, 1932, pp. 3–7.
25 See Atkins, 2010, pp. 114–7. This argument, on the conquest by this Japanese empress called Empress Zingu, was included in school textbooks in Korea throughout the colonial rule. See also Government-General of Chosen, *Hutsū gakkō Kokushi: jidōyō* [National History for Primary School Children] (1922).
26 Government-General of Korea, "Chōsen sōtokubu hakubutsukan oyobi koseki chōsa kaiyō," April 1925.
27 In 1915, two Korean intellectuals, Park Eun-sik and Eo Yun-jeok, managed to publish books on Korean history, putting emphasis on a Dangun-centered perspective of history. In particular, an exiled historian, Park, in his book published in China, *Hanguk tongsa* [The Tragic History of Korea], argued with the Japanese scholars who emphasised the ancient relation between Japan and Korea. His book was smuggled into Korea, and the colonial authorities, who were afraid of its influence, put forward their own compilation of Korean history (Jeong, 2001, pp. 13–16).
28 Three golden crowns were excavated by GGM in 1921, 1924 and 1926, respectively.
29 *The Dong-A Ilbo*, 7 July, 15 July, 16 July, 10 August, 15 October, 23 October and 19 November 1923, 10 July and 10 August 1924, 24 September, 2 October, 24 October, 28 October, 28 October, 30 October and 7 December 1925, and 16 January 1926; *The Chosunilbo*, 15 August, 29 October and 23 November 1923, 5 January, 8 July, and 5 August 1924, and 4 September 1925.
30 Anon., "Gojeok bojon gwa beopgyu e gwanhayeo [On the Preservation of Historical Remains and the Related Act]," *The Dong-A Ilbo*, 29 November 1929.
31 Anon., "Sillasidae gukbo dosil [National Treasures of the Silla Period Stolen]," *Maeil sinbo*, 13 December 1927.
32 *The Dong-A Ilbo*, 4 December 1926, 5 December 1926 and 6 December 1926.
33 *The Dong-A Ilbo*, 16 September 1925.
34 *Maeil sinbo*, 26 February 1933.
35 The following remark by Yi Hang-gu, the Minister of the Office of the Yi Royal Household symbolically explains the authority that GGM enjoyed throughout the colonial rule. "In 1938, the YHM changed its name to the Yi Royal Household Museum of Art in order to follow the trend of the era and to avoid competition with the Government-General Museum." See "Jo [Preface]," *Liōke bijutskan chinretsu nihonbijutshin zuroku* [Catalogue of the Japanese Artworks of the Yi Royal Household Museum of Art], 1938.
36 *The Dong-A Ilbo*, 26 August 1937.
37 Shiobara Tokisaburo, "Gojeok aehoil e daehaya [On the Penchant Day for Historical Remains]," *Maeil sinbo*, 12 September 1937.
38 GGM, *Kodai naisen kankei siryō tokubetsu tenran annai* [A Guide to the Special Exhibition, Relations between Korea and Japan in the Ancient Period], Seoul, 1938.
39 Oh Bong-bin, "Seohwa goldong ui sujangga [Collectors of Paintings and Antiquities: Upon the Disposal of the Park Chang-hun Collection]," *The Dong-A Ilbo*, 1 May 1940.
40 Kim argues that Go established Korean art history as a modern discipline through conducting research into material elements of Korean history and art. Kim adds that Go criticised Sekino's research on Korean art as just a register of cultural relics.

2 Independence, the National Museum and the US

On 15 August 1945, the emperor of Japan surrendered to the allied powers. To Koreans, the emperor's proclamation meant liberation from Japanese colonial rule. However, Japan's surrender to the allied powers did not guarantee prompt reestablishment of an independent government in Korea. Instead, the US and the USSR armies advanced into Korea, south and north of the 38th Parallel, respectively, according to the instrument of surrender signed between the allied powers and Japan on 2 September 1945. On 9 September, the US forces in the 24th Corps of the 10th Army advanced on Seoul and established the US Army Military Government in Korea (hereafter, USAMGIK). This lasted for three years until the establishment of the government of the Republic of Korea south of the 38th Parallel.

Under USAMGIK, South Korea began to undergo drastic changes, strongly influenced by the US, which was emerging as one of the two superpowers after the Second World War. They preferred to present themselves as pioneers of democracy and freedom. However, Korea's strategic value to the US was still somewhat vague in comparison with Japan's in the latter part of the 1940s. Furthermore, their lack of understanding of, and interest in, the current state and background of Korea often made their efforts inconsistent and even ineffective (Armstrong, 2003, p. 73). Throughout the 1950s, American ambitions in Korea gradually became more practical and concrete, as South Korea's geo-strategic value as a bastion of the American world order increased after the Korean War.

Meanwhile, liberation gave Koreans from diverse fields many opportunities. Only now did Korea secure the political, social and cultural space within which to establish its identity. Only now did Korea – and in particular NMK – find a role in acts of identity-making that sought to extract Korean identity from Japanese colonial impositions. In this regard, it is noteworthy that USAMGIK established the National Museum on 3 December 1945, about three months after the end of the Japanese occupation of Korea.

Requisition of the Government-General Museum and Kim Chewon

With the unconditional surrender of the Japanese empire on 15 August 1945, the Government-General began to contact reliable Korean leaders. Yeo Un-hyeong (1886–1947), a popular moderate leftist political leader, was asked to head an interim administrative committee to maintain law and order. Yeo accepted that offer and quickly organised the Committee for the Preparation of Korean Independence. Yeo and his committee set about establishing a government to replace the Japanese Government-General.

This included requisitioning GGM. This museum attracted the interest of Kim Chewon (1909–1990), who had obtained a doctoral degree in education from Munich University in 1934 (Kim, 1992, p. 50). Afterwards, Kim had assisted Professor Karl Hentze (1883–1975) at Gent University in Belgium, where he spent five years translating East Asian art and archaeology literatures into German as well as assisting Hentze in his research. This experience led Kim to the East Asian literature. After returning to Korea in 1940, Kim taught German as a part-time lecturer at Bosung College in Seoul until the liberation (Kim, 1992, pp. 54–6).

Two days after the liberation, Kim resolved to put into practice his plan to take over GGM. According to Arimitsu Kyoichi (1907–2011), a Japanese manager of GGM and an archaeologist, on 17 August 1945, Kim had a meeting to discuss the takeover of the museum with Arimitsu. Interestingly, Kim told Arimitsu, "I'm here at the request of the Committee for the Preparation of Korean Independence, although I'm not a member of the committee" (Arimitsu, 1985a, pp. 223–6).

Arimitsu, who had been afraid of the drastic changes that took place following 15 August, was able to trust Kim. Through this mutual trust, Kim strove to get as much information as possible from Arimitsu. Afterwards, Kim made a visit to two local museums of GGM, at Buyeo and Gyeongju, for their requisition (Kim, 1992, p. 83). Kim and Arimitsu awaited the arrival of the US occupation army in Seoul, and they discussed the management of GGM and pending problems regarding Korean archaeology.

American ambition and the opening of the National Museum

On 1 September 1945, the US occupation army defined its mission as the demolishment of militarism; the disarmament of Japanese troops in Korea; the inspiration of democratic tendency and process; the encouragement of liberal political, economic and social institution; and the creation of which could guarantee the advent of a responsible country with which the United Nations could keep peace.[1] The Americans seemed to be quite sure that they could secure a stable support base for their interest in the Korean peninsula through the accomplishment of this mission. Indeed, USAMGIK aimed to be seen as pioneers of a new standard of civilisation, with qualities such as democracy and freedom.

With regard to this foreign policy, the US army had already set out its basic policy on cultural relics in occupied regions in a field manual.[2] In this manual, USAMGIK reasserted its policy on cultural objects and installations in Korea: "Historical, cultural and religious object & installations will be carefully preserved and protected."[3] According to a report forwarded to the Director of the Bureau of Education, the Bureau of Education of USAMGIK, in this context, set it as one of its "immediate needs" to "appropriate [a] budget for reopening and operating of the national museum" in terms of the field of arts and monuments.[4]

On 11 September, when USAMGIK took over the Bureau of Education of the Government-General, Captain Earl Lockard, the new director of the Bureau of Education of USAMGIK, set about organising the bureau. One of the most difficult challenges that USAMGIK faced then was to find the right people to fill posts in the military government. Kim, who could speak English and had a doctoral degree, was considered to be a very competent person for the post. Lockard took Kim into his confidence, employed him at the bureau on 21 September, and appointed him as director of the National Museum on 26 September.

Indeed, Kim was gaining trust from his American bosses. His suggestion in relation to reopening and operating the former GGM attracted their attention, and some of the important issues raised by Kim were included in a bureau report dated 3 October 1945. In his letter, Kim suggested that a separate government bureau for the museum be considered.[5] The letter reveals that Kim had grown aware of the main focus of the cultural policies of USAMGIK and could utilise it to acquire what he wanted. Captain Eugene Knez (1916–2010), who was assigned to the bureau on 29 November and later became the director of the Department of Culture, also had a high opinion of Kim's ability and enthusiasm for the job. Knez recollected that he was a well-qualified person of the sort who could hardly be found in South Korea at that time (Kim, 1991, pp. 100–7).

Remarkably, USAMGIK established a post of director for the museum, although the Government-General did not place such a post in GGM, which had been annexed to the Department of Social Education under the Bureau of Education in the Government-General. Furthermore, the museum was unorganised. USAMGIK established three sections, general affairs, curatorial affairs and exhibitions, respectively, each under a director.

The military government wanted to open the museum as soon as possible. This was how the government planned to disseminate the American values of independence or freedom to Koreans. In other words, those values were intended as vital to explaining the American standard of civilisation. It was remarkable that USAMGIK called the museum "national" even before an independent Korean government was established. This action shows that USAMGIK was trying to win the trust of Koreans by presenting them with the hope of an independent country. That is, the military government intended to wipe out the negative image of military occupation through cultural institutions.

In order to achieve this, the military government encouraged the Bureau of Education to reopen the museum. The bureau decided that Arimitsu should remain in office and help Kim, who did not have any experienced Korean staff members to manage the museum (Arimitsu, 1985a, p. 229). The Department of Education was already planning for its reopening. The report included very detailed plans, such as the immediate repair of buildings and walkways in the museum, and the restoration and preservation of the museum garden.[6] On 2 October, Lieutenant Paul Mitchell, the chief of the Department of Culture, ordered Kim and Arimitsu to reopen the museum (Arimitsu, 1985a, p. 229).

It was Arimitsu who took the lead in the restoration of the permanent exhibition (Arimitsu, 1985a, pp. 232–3). According to his memoirs, he restored the former exhibition of GGM, giving training to the newly employed Korean curatorial members. On 3 December 1945, the National Museum under USAMGIK was opened. The same artefacts displayed in GGM represented a totally different meaning in the National Museum: the cultural identity of an independent nation, not the local culture of the Japanese empire.

The first issue of NMK's *Gwanbo* (national museum gazette), in describing the opening of NMK, stated, "NMK made a clean sweep of Japanese manners and changed the entire look of the museum."[7] However, it does not seem that this was more than the elimination of the Japanese language from museum labels throughout the museum. Above all, the former chief of GGM took the lead in the exhibition. Even Kim might not have been able to find problems in the narratives that GGM had constructed. This explains why Kim's criticism of the Japanese narrative and its problems cannot be found in his memoirs. Although GGM was criticised for its "lack of understanding of management and facilities of the museum because of colonial cultural policies based on militarism" and for "not taking care of the museum during the war,"[8] there was not any concrete criticism of GGM's activities.

Instead, interestingly, NMK gave GGM considerable credit for "mobilising the best scholars in excavation projects in centres of old cultural relics in Korea, publishing the excavation reports for the academic world through research of the excavated artefacts, and giving publicity to them even within the Western world."[9] This evaluation meant that NMK had to accept Japanese authority with regard to the discovery and interpretation of Korean material culture. It is thought to have been in this context that Kim stated in his memoirs that Japanese scholars should be given credit for publishing a series of reports on the old relics of Korea, when even Koreans did not know their old relics (Kim, 1991, p. 161).

This demonstrates that Japanese scholars had the upper hand in the discovery and interpretation of Korean material culture during the colonial period; Korean scholars were not able to participate in these projects.[10] As a result, it was not easy for them to organise their own perspectives on their own material culture. The US military governor, Major General Archibald V. Arnold's comment at the opening ceremony of NMK reveals a great deal; he stated, "Koreans need to make much effort in order to preserve old art relics which would be a foundation for the creation of Korean culture, and give publicity to their genuine values."[11]

NMK's first step for independent management and its limits

In his foreword of the first issue of *Gwanbo*, Kim defined NMK's mission as stepping further in contributing to establishing an independent country in the field of culture, being based on the premise that "It has been one and a half years since the liberation. However, we have a long way to independence. … Our management of the museum has not got into its stride."[12] Until April 1946, NMK had under its control two local municipal museums, Gongju Museum and Gaeseong Museum, making a total of 4 branches in its network, including two former branch museums of GGM in Gyeongju and Buyeo.

Now, NMK had a nationwide organisation, and *Gwanbo* proudly remarked that:

> by becoming an independent institution under the supervision of the Department of Education, NMK secured a status as a museum which represents our country, [that] by securing four branch museums, NMK could intensify a function as a museum centred on history and art [and that] by establishing three sections, of general affairs, curatorial affairs and the exhibition in the main museum in Seoul, NMK has constructed a foundation for future development.[13]

He also pointed out that all of these functions could be executed only by securing "manpower with the right talent."

For NMK, which was striving to secure an independent capacity for managing the museum, acquiring academic staff was a pending issue. However, there were only a few Korean academics in the fields of art history and archaeology. Unlike Korean history and language, which drew much interest from promoters of the cultural independence movement, the material culture of Korea did not receive much attention. GGM had never employed Korean curatorial staff members. To make it worse, there were no Korean archaeologists experienced in excavation, and no Korean art historians educated at a university level, at the time of the liberation. In addition, there were many posts now available in universities, colleges and government departments after the Japanese vacated their posts. As Kim recalled, any graduate of a prestigious university could have chances with these posts, but the museum was not a workplace interesting enough to attract them at that time (Kim, 1991, p. 161).

Kim tried to find university graduates in adjacent fields or from renowned universities. As can be seen in Table 2.1, it took some time to appoint some university graduates to the main museum in Seoul, and most of them did not have any background in Korean art history or archaeology. It was not until the latter part of 1947 that NMK secured a considerable workforce for curatorial affairs (Figure 2.1). However, in the branch museums it was best to employ the former administrative clerks who had worked with Japanese directors. Jin Hong-seop, who was appointed as the director of Gaeseong branch museum, was the only university graduate assigned to a local museum.

Thus, it took long time to secure the curatorial staff, and they had to accumulate academic capability from scratch. It was for this reason that USAMGIK asked Arimitsu stay in Korea longer so that he could provide guidance to the new Korean curatorial staff. For Kim, who was seeking measures to secure independent capability of investigating Korean material culture, the presence of Arimitsu was indispensable. It seems likely that Kim persuaded his American bosses to make Arimitsu remain in Korea.[14]

Kim thought that GGM had a strong tradition of excavation and research. He believed that Korean curators should build on this capability. His efforts led to a trip to Gyeongju in March 1946 for the selection of an ancient tomb for excavation. At this time, Arimitsu recommended a tomb which he had already recognised previously. The then director of Department of Culture, Knez, who was a graduate of the Department of Anthropology at the University of New Mexico, also endeavoured to actualise this excavation plan along with Kim (Knez, 1997, pp. 27–30). Consequently, USAMGIK publicised the plan in *Stars and Stripes*, a bulletin of the US armed forces (Arimitsu, 1985c, p. 197). Presumably, USAMGIK judged that the excavation could attract positive opinion from the South Korean public and contribute to stabilising the present South Korean society.

Table 2.1 Newly employed curatorial staff at NMK in the latter part of the 1940s*

Name	*Academic background*	*Date of employment*	*Others*
Kim Chewon (1909–1990)	University of Munich Education, PhD	21 September 1945	1945–1970: Director of NMK
Lim Cheon (1908–1965)	Tokyo Fine Arts School (dropout), draftsman	October 1945	
Lee Hong-jik (1909–1970)	Tokyo Imperial Univ. History, BA	20 December 1945	1958–1970: Prof. of Korea Univ.
Seo Gap-rok (?–1949)	Yonhee College	1 May 1946	
Chang Uk-jin (1917–1990)	Imperial Art School, painter	Before February 1947	Resignation on 30 September 1947
Kim Won-yong (1922–1993)	Keijo Imperial Univ. History, BA	1 February 1947	1970–1971: Director of NMK 1961–1987: Prof. of Seoul National Univ.
Jin Hong-seop (1918–2010)	Meiji Univ. Economics, BA	1 April 1947	Resignation in 1963 1963–1983: Prof. of Ewha Univ.
Hwang Su-yeong (1918–2011)	Tokyo Imperial Univ. Economics, BA	1 August 1947	Resignation in 1950 1971–1974: Director of NMK 1956–1986: Prof. of Dongguk Univ.
Min Cheon-sik (?–1950?)	Waseda Univ, Unknown, BA	1 October 1947	
Choi Sunu** (1916–1984)	Songdo Middle School	15 April 1946	1974–1984: Director of NMK

* Compiled from NMK, *Gwanbo*, vol.1 to vol.8, 1947–1949; Kim Chewon, 1991, pp. 7–69; Kim Chewon, 1992, pp. 83–110.

** Choi was transferred to the main museum in Seoul from Gaeseong branch museum on 31 December 1949.

Surprisingly, this month-long excavation in Gyeongju was successful. This 15-century old, small, Silla tomb, which was named "Houchong (Hou tomb)" after the inscriptions on a vessel found there, did not produce many artefacts; however, among them was a vessel with important inscriptions suggesting a specific international relationship between two major ancient

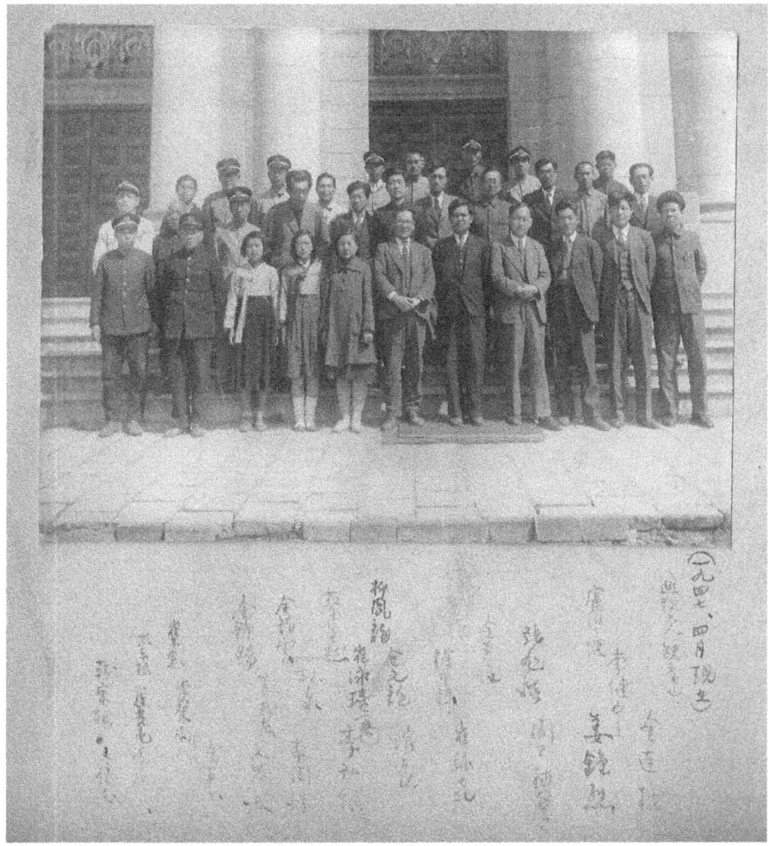

Figure 2.1 NMK's staff members (April 1947). With kind permission from Professor Kim Lena.

kingdoms, Goguryeo and Silla, in the 6th century (NMK, 1948). This "first" excavation by Koreans was literally a great success (Figure 2.2).

Although this excavation was guided by a Japanese archaeologist and sponsored by the American military government, it was the first time that Koreans excavated their material culture for themselves. This excavation attracted the attention of academics as well as the press. In a contribution to *The Seoul Shinmun*, Kim described this excavation as a truly nationwide project, saying that "almost all scholars related to Korean studies assembled in Gyeongju, as the centre of academic circle temporarily moved to this place."[15]

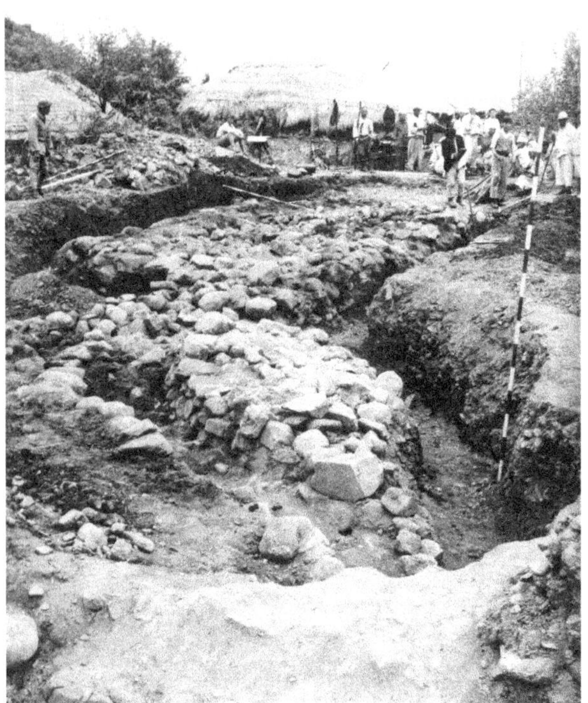

Figure 2.2 NMK's first excavation in Gyeongju in 1946. With kind permission from NMK.

Museum staff members were deeply moved by the fact that they had conducted the excavation with their own hands, produced excellent results and reported the results in the Korean language.[16] They felt that they were learning how to discover evidence of their material culture through excavation. They could also be proud of overcoming the colonial situation in which discoveries of Korean material culture through archaeological investigation had been monopolised by the Japanese. Indeed, they were, through their material culture, seeking for a way to contribute to building an independent country.

Another important task of the curatorial staff members of NMK was to study the concrete contents of Korean material culture. As shown above, they were not specialised in this field, even though they had quite an excellent academic background. A study group was organised at NMK on 3 August 1946. The main purpose of this group was to "enlighten them about archaeology."[17] On Saturdays, they took courses on specific subjects provided by the specialists and presented what they had learned through reading on a specific field. This study group also attracted the participation of the National Museum of Anthropology and Incheon Municipal Museum.[18] This attempt to study material culture suggests that the curatorial staff realised that is was important to understand the meaning and value of the museum collection. NMK staff members were encouraged to join other academic societies. Kim took the lead in participating in academic societies. He was an organiser of both the Korean Anthropological Society in May 1946 and the Institute of Korean Formative Arts Culture in March 1947.[19]

Kim therefore laid the groundwork for the discovery of and research into Korean material culture. However, it was not possible in the short term to criticise and replace the colonial narrative which the Japanese had constructed for more than 40 years. Although a couple of books on Korean history were published by nationalist historians in the latter part of the 1940s, they were not familiar with Korean material culture. Furthermore, it was evident that Korean material culture could not be reorganised without the systematic accumulation and research of material evidences. Kim realised this, and therefore considered the "ethnic nation" to be the main agent of building Korean's new country. However, he did not agree to absolutising and mythifying the concept, without its basis on historical evidence.[20] His contribution to *The Seoul Shinmun* in July 1947 shows his understanding of the ethnic nation at that time:

> A nation that has a long history is entitled to have pride in its past. In truth, do we have anything to show the world at the moment? If we have something, it would be our accomplishments from our past toward overall Eastern Culture. We should realise that our nation's past entitles us to a status of an independent country. We should keep in mind that our nation's past and our cultural capability, neither the Cairo Declaration nor the Moscow Conference among foreign ministers, qualify us for independence.[21]

He emphasised the cultural capacity of a nation as a qualification for its independence. In this regard, cultural accomplishments would have to be discovered, preserved and interpreted for the independence of a nation. However, what he wanted to focus on for this goal was concrete artefacts to prove the cultural identity of Korea, not the notion of an ethnic nation as vague political propaganda. He was discreet in putting forward the notion of the ethnic nation in explaining the projects of NMK.[22] However, he was also wise enough not to be criticised for his attitude by the government or the public. This was partly because material culture itself attracted little attention, and because the notion of an ethnic nation, ironically, was considerably losing its political potential owing to ideological conflicts in South Korea after the liberation in 1945.[23]

Meanwhile, Kim had to deal with both the demands and problems of USAMGIK. It was evident that the Department of Education of USAMGIK tried to secure its image as a protector of Korean cultural heritage through a series of projects, such as the reorganisation of the Committee of the Preservation of Cultural Relics, cataloguing of the important relics, opening of the National Museum and creation of the National Museum of Anthropology (literally, National Museum of the "ethnic nation"). Furthermore, the department also attempted to draw up the list of cultural artefacts stolen by Japanese during colonial rule. The department also sponsored the building of a 10-storey pagoda located in a very popular park in Seoul with the assistance of the US military engineering unit. Through this, the department was trying to make Koreans positively disposed to USAMGIK by showing that they could contribute to stabilising the political situation of South Korean society.

USAMGIK, however, also had clear limits in the practice of its policies. First of all, the Department of Culture had no strong voice in the military government. Some actions of USAMGIK often made South Korean intellectuals doubt that they had a sincere respect for Korean cultural relics, or even for Koreans in general. In March 1946, USAMGIK was criticised for trying to build a military barracks at the site of a palace from the Goryeo dynasty (936–1392) in Gaeseong. This construction was stopped after an inspection by Langdon Warner (1881–1955) of the Fogg Museum of Oriental Art, Harvard University, who was then working at the Arts and Monuments Section of General Headquarters, the Supreme Commander for the Allied Powers (HQ/SCAP) in Tokyo.

In August 1946, USAMGIK pushed ahead another construction, the housing for dependants of American military staff in a vacant ground of Gyeongbokgung Palace, where the National Museum was located. When underground structures of demolished buildings were found there, USAMGIK faced criticism from South Korean newspapers (Kim, 1991, pp. 19–22). Kim Chewon and Song Seok-ha (1904–1948, Director of the National Museum of Anthropology and Chairman of the Committee of Preservation of Cultural Relics) also suggested reconsideration.

This issue reminded South Koreans of the destruction of the palace by Japanese during their colonial rule. And Kim had to be reprimanded by the military government for the reason that Kim assisted in publicising the construction to the press (Kim, 1991, pp. 19–22). More importantly, NMK had to close down for about 9 months, from 29 August 1946 to 25 June 1947, for the convenience of the construction, and this also became another target of criticism.[24] This inconsistency in museum policy shows that the culture section of USAMGIK could never have a strong voice in the military government. It can be said that on this issue USAMGIK failed even to meet their own standards. Although some American officers assigned to the culture section of the military government showed enthusiasm for a series of cultural projects, including the opening of NMK, USAMGIK's priority in its policies was also evident. It is in this context that Armstrong argued, "In addition, if the occupation of Korea was an afterthought of US military planners, then culture was an afterthought of an afterthought" (Armstrong, 2003, p. 73).

In addition, the response from South Korean society was an important issue for Kim. In the latter part of the 1940s, there was not much consideration made for material culture among most South Koreans. South Korean society was experiencing drastic political and social changes and disorder over the future of a new country. Most political elites could not afford to focus on the potential of material culture for building a new modern nation-state. NMK was struggling to secure a foundation for the management of the museum, but the response from political and social circles was minimal. With the exception of some military government officials, no political leaders visited NMK until the first president of the Republic of Korea, Rhee Syngman (1875–1965), did so in February 1949.[25] South Korean political leaders in those days rarely sought to capitalise on the political value of material culture. In most cases, it was not until some cultural objects were damaged or stolen that artefacts could draw the attention of South Koreans. Although South Koreans had gradually been recognising these cultural objects as treasures of the ethnic nation since the colonial period, it can be said that a sincere interest in these objects was definitely not a priority.

It was the Americans who tried to utilise the political potential of cultural objects of the occupied area. USAMGIK's pre-emptive action, such as the prompt opening of the national museum, can be said to be a typical example. Meanwhile, once President Harry S. Truman declared his doctrine to block the expansion of communist power in Greece and Turkey in March 1947, the struggle for power between the US and the USSR intensified. The Korean peninsula, now occupied by both powers, gradually became an arena for competition over the superiority of ideologies and politics. It was around this time that the Rockefeller Foundation sent its assistant director of the Humanities Division, Charles B. Fahs (1908–1980), to South Korea (Kim, 1991, p. 56).

Director Kim's visit to the US and its meaning

Director Kim and another staff member, Kim Won-yong (the future director of NMK, 1970–1971 in office), were invited by the Rockefeller Foundation to study in the US for one year beginning in April 1948. The US government was focusing on exchange of human resources and construction of knowledge networks as an effective means to disseminate American ideas and institutions across South Korea. It is worth noting that US-based private foundations such as the Rockefeller Foundation collaborated with US government agencies in cultural activities (Parmar, 2012, pp. 257–60). It was against this background that Fahs came to South Korea in spring 1947, to choose the fields in which American support was needed. Fahs placed priority in training young Korean journalists, and decided to show ten journalists the present condition of the American media. Kim obtained the opportunity to explain to Fahs the many difficulties facing NMK, including a budget deficit, poor facilities and lack of professional manpower. This meeting led to the foundation inviting the two staff members to the US (Kim, 1991, pp. 56 and 168).[26]

During his stay in the US, Kim visited many American museums and met key scholars in the field of East Asian studies, especially art and archaeology. As a result, he became a key figure in the cultural exchange between South Korea and the US. Kim, who could communicate in English, was the right person to be the main gateway of academic information related to Korean material culture and East Asian culture. Kim thought much of meeting with Langdon Warner, who was working at the Fogg Museum at Harvard University, because he considered Warner to be the senior scholar in the field of East Asian art and archaeology in the US. Kim wanted his guidance as much as possible. At the first meeting, on May 1946, they discussed pending issues concerning NMK as well as Kim's plans during his stay in the US (Kim, 1991, p. 223).

At the same time, Professor Alfred Salmony (1890–1958), a Jewish German scholar at New York University, had been acquainted with Kim from the 1930s, and had started with Hentze *Artibus Asiae*, a journal on East Asian Culture.[27] Salmony, then editor-in-chief of the journal, introduced Korean culture to a wider audience. Thanks to his favour, Kim could publish a report on the first excavation of NMK to *Artibus Asiae*.[28] In June 1950, Salmony came to South Korea with five other American professors to give lectures on several topics, an event which was organised as an academic exchange programme sponsored by the Rockefeller Foundation.[29] An overseas special exhibition of Korean cultural objects in the US was also discussed during Kim's visit. Warner put forward the necessity of the exhibition to Kim (Kim, 1991, p. 109). The Rockefeller Foundation also recommended that Kim discuss this project with Robert P. Griffing Jr., the director of the Honolulu Academy of Arts (1947–1963 in office), on his return to Korea in December 1948 (Kim, 1991, pp. 109–11).[30]

Kim's visit to the US gave Kim many opportunities. He surveyed several issues related to the management of NMK, such as system cataloguing and collection storing. Kim learned about the role of museums as public educational institutions. He paid special attention to the fact that public education played a big part in American museums. He was impressed by public education programmes at the Museum of Fine Art, Boston, as well as the utilisation of projectors and movies at the Buffalo Museum of Science.

Kim commented in the foreword to his memoirs that he thought his visit to the US was very meaningful (Kim, 1991, p. 4). This suggests that the standards of American museums and their networks gave him good guidance and support in his own personal life. He especially realised the importance of public education, as he was trying to help the public in his newly independent country become familiar with their material culture. Through this visit, Kim was able to build a network with American academics, and he became a key figure in that network. This meant that US scholars could acquire a stable ground for securing academic materials related to East Asian material culture,[31] and that Korean academics not only secured a key route by which to introduce Korean material culture into American academic society but also opened a possibility of continued financial support from US-based private foundations.[32]

An important change which Kim's visit to the US brought to NMK was the introduction of an education programme for the public in May 1949. This programme, entitled "art lectures," was organised for the purpose of "enlightening the public."[33] According to *Gwanbo*, NMK defined as one of its important tasks to "diffuse related knowledge to the public in general, especially students." For this goal, NMK set teachers of primary and secondary schools as main targets of this lecture course. The first course consisted of six lectures, and each lecture was delivered by lecturers, from either inside or outside of NMK, every Saturday afternoon from 7 May to 11 June, 1949. This course covered Buddhist sculpture, Buddhist pagodas, porcelain, woodcraft and East Asian painting.[34] Until 1950, NMK held this course three times in total, and each course attracted 20 to 30 teachers from around the Seoul area. Noteworthily, those lecturers were aided by projectors that Kim had brought from the US (Kim, 1991, pp. 32–3).

The Korean War and the setback to NMK

The outbreak of the Korean War set back the efforts made by NMK. All of the collections and most of the staff members in Seoul were left under the rule of North Korea only three days after the outbreak of war on 25 June 1950. Kim Chewon was forced into hiding in Seoul. Kim Yong-tae, from the Committee for Material Culture of the North Korean Cabinet, took over

NMK. However, the counter-attack by UN forces, led by US forces, forced the North Koreans to give up Seoul and retreat on 27 September 1950.

Meanwhile, with the People's Republic of China's forces participating in the war in support of North Korea, things quickly changed. Kim Chewon decided to move major collections to Busan, a port city on the south-eastern coast, before Seoul would be retaken by the North Korean forces on 4 January 1951. However, it was not easy to activate this evacuation plan. The South Korean government was concerned about public unrest and so was slow in implementing the evacuation plan. Eventually, the government had to permit the evacuation in order to not lose "national treasures" to North Korea. At the same time, the US side had more things to take into consideration. The US government remembered the international criticism it had to face when they moved the collections in the Kaiser Friedrich Museum in Berlin to the US after the end of the Second World War, even though this was for the purpose of protecting the collection (Kim, 1991, pp. 79–80).[35]

Kim made an appeal for help to Eugene Knez, managing chief of a local branch of the US Information Services (USIS) at the US Embassy in South Korea. Knez, the former chief of the Department of Culture, USAMGIK, in 1946, risked criticism both from the US government and from the communists for helping NMK and the Deoksugung Art Gallery to evacuate their collections. He sponsored transportation – trucks and trains – for the evacuation to Busan. He even provided a temporary place to keep the collections in the Busan branch of the USIS (Knez, 1997, pp. 41–5). His help was essential to the protection of major collections of NMK, and Kim kept immeasurable faith in the US side.

The seesaw battles during the war led the South Korean government to express concerns about the collections that had been evacuated to Busan. In 1951, South Korean president Rhee Syngman even directed to evacuate those collections to the US.[36] However, the US government was reluctant to accept his request on the same diplomatic, strategic reasons stated before. Instead, Griffing, the director of the Honolulu Academy of Arts, volunteered to take custody of the collections. NMK even set about repacking for the evacuation to Honolulu, but negotiations for a truce made it come to a halt. Until the signing of the truce in July 1953, NMK had to stay in Busan, preserving the collections and setting up small-scale exhibitions of traditional and modern Korean paintings (NMK, 2006, p. 49).

The return of NMK to Seoul and the establishment of the museum mission

After the truce was signed on 27 July 1953, NMK returned to Seoul along with the government, with the main collections remaining in Busan. After its return, NMK had to find another building, because the president, under the guise of the preservation of the palace, directed NMK to leave the Gyeongbokgung Palace, in which its main building was located. The three-year-long war, which left about 1.3 million casualties on the South Korean side alone (Eckert, 1990c, p. 345), did not allow for museum activities to receive priority over the recovery from the immense war damage. NMK had to move to the building of the former National Museum of Anthropology, which had been absorbed into a branch museum of NMK for an administrative simplification right after the outbreak of the war. NMK managed to open its permanent exhibition with artefacts that remained in Seoul on May 1954. However, NMK's activities could not avoid being reduced to the minimum as a result of the limited manpower and deficient budget, for the time being. In the same year, NMK had to follow another unreasonable order: to hand over the building to the military authorities, which clearly showed the priority of the decision making of the government in those days.

Kim managed to meet President Rhee and succeed in persuading him to allow NMK to use Seokjojeon Hall at Deoksugung Palace, in which Japanese artworks had been displayed during the colonial period. The fact that the president himself had to decide whether to reconstruct a national museum or not showed the miserable difficulties that South Korea experienced after the war. Kim heartily expressed his gratitude in that Rhee make a resolute decision to reconstruct NMK there, stating that Rhee's long exile in Western countries had made him understand the importance of the museum (Kim, 1991, pp. 86–93). In 1955, NMK opened its permanent exhibition at Seokjojeon Hall, concentrating on the normalisation of functions of NMK. However, the majority of the major collections were still in Busan because of the continued threat to national security.

During this difficult period, NMK did take one particular step to revive NMK: the establishment of the museum mission. This mission, which comprised three articles, is thought to have been established from late 1953 to early 1955, and was first recorded as the museum's mission on a business report as of February 1955.[37] Even though its date of establishment is unsure, this mission is considered to be a milestone in NMK's history. Both criticising the management of GGM and reflecting its activities since its foundation in 1945, NMK tried to define its mission precisely and set out its vision of a national museum of the fledging state, the Republic of Korea, recognising that NMK should now contribute to the construction of nation building and reparation of the devastating damage from the war.[38]

The mission can be broken down into independent management, the enlightenment of the public and the development of knowledge and art. It was intended to propose concrete ways for finding a cultural identity of an independent nation as main agents of the discourse on material culture. These ways were to break through the authoritarian management of GGM, to enlighten the Korean public, and to develop knowledge and art. This establishment of the museum's mission is thought to have given concrete method and shape at the time to the revival of NMK after the war, and to NMK's mission as proposed by Kim in 1947: that is, to lay a foundation of the independent nation promptly in the field of culture.[39] In short, this beginning stage of NMK was a period in which NMK organised its operational system as a cultural institution and searched for a direction and method of development. The war and its damage delayed NMK's development and restricted the activities of NMK. However, its mission and vision for the future began to take shape. It was around this time that a discussion on the overseas special exhibition of Korean art in Korea resumed between Korea and the US.

Overseas exhibition and nation building

The chance to draw the attention of South Korean leaders to Korean material culture came from diplomatic need in the latter part of the 1950s. US assistance to the South Korean government was essential for national security and reconstruction following the damage resulting from the Korean War. Furthermore, South Korea, which stood at the forefront of the Cold War on behalf of the US, attempted to attract as much aid as it could from the US, leading to occasional diplomatic tensions. It was in this context that NMK's first large-scale overseas exhibition of Korean culture toured eight cities in the US between 1957 and 1959.[40]

The US considered East Asia as an outpost of the Cold War and intervened in that area very actively (Cha, 2006, pp. 258–61). In 1950, the US intervened in Korea to push back a North Korean invasion. After this, the US signed a mutual defence treaty with South Korea in 1953, and "maintained tens of thousands of American troops' and even tactical nuclear weapons on the Korean peninsula" (Eckert, 1990b, p. 395). In the first half of the 1950s, the US constructed an international order in opposition to the USSR (Heo, 2008, p. 326). In order to maintain a stable, pro-American regime in South Korea, the US started to change direction from purely military aid to political and economic assistance, which resulted in the necessity of the internal health of this pro-American and anti-communist regime (Lee, 2006, p. 551).

Their consideration for constructing a stable regime in South Korea included cultural aspects such as helping it to affirm its national identity through material culture. As Heo pointed out, the US was willing to characterise itself as the nation that supported other nations' aspirations for national freedom in the course of its competition with the USSR (Heo, 2008, pp. 326–8).[41] It was in this context that the US pushed ahead with a series of cultural projects towards South Korea under the name of cultural exchange. The American side also took the initiative in that discussion.

It was the Americans rather than the Koreans who which raised the necessity of the exhibition; this exhibition was possible because the Americans, rather than the Koreans, wanted it.

Although the US took the initiative from the beginning of the project, the South Korean government was by far the more active in expressing its expectations through this touring exhibition. South Korean officials and politicians expected to accrue both practical and cultural profits from the event. South Korea hoped to improve its image through cultural objects, and, by doing so, to maximise aid from the US. Both aspects were expected to contribute to securing a national identity. In other words, South Korean leaders thought that showing off the essence of Korean material culture in the US could be a soft and useful tactic in securing a cultural and political citizenship in a world order presided over by the US. A further outcome expected from the US exhibition was to recover national dignity following the disgrace experienced during Japanese colonial rule (Hahn, 2012, 162–4). The US was deemed to be the right country to guarantee Korea's national dignity and respect its national identity (Jang, 2016, pp. 457–60).

In 1954, the South Korean government organised the Overseas Exhibition Committee which consisted of 16 members; the mission was to advise on general affairs, including the selection of artefacts for the exhibition. NMK was determined to prepare a good exhibition showcasing Korean culture in the US. Director Kim made efforts to select as many masterpieces as possible to represent Korean culture. In September 1954, the committee finished the preliminary selection of 306 items before the American members of the selection committee (Ministry of Education, 1960, p. 1). Two members of the American committee, Alan Priest (1898–1969) of the Metropolitan Museum of Art and Robert T. Paine Jr. (1900–1965) of the Museum of Fine Arts in Boston, made the final selection of 193 items for this first overseas exhibition.

The American curators' selection not only surprised Korean members but also disappointed them, especially in regard to their choice of paintings. The US curators were specialised in Chinese and Japanese art and did not always have the same opinions as their Korean counterparts, even with regard to Korean painters such as Sin Yun-bok (1758–?) and Kim Hong-do (1745–?), whom Koreans considered great masters (Kim, 1991, p. 112). The US curators preferred artefacts which could show differences from other Asian cultures, namely Chinese culture, and therefore demonstrate the independence of Korean culture. Members of the American selection committee placed a priority on the response of American audiences and therefore are thought to have preferred artefacts which could effectively explain the independence of Korean culture from East Asian culture.

An interesting point to note is that the American curators were more active and determined to find things genuinely Korean than were the Korean committee members. However, they overlooked the fact that the Koreans considered Chinese civilisation to be their important standard, even though they had transformed it and created things in Korean ways. The US curators actually lost some objective perspective on East Asian art in terms of the influence and exchange of culture in East Asia. Their preoccupation that Korean culture should have only Korean things can be argued to have been influenced partly by the political situation. The US government wanted to build a stable state in South Korea. And this state also needed to be culturally independent. The existence of China in the communist bloc must also have been a considerable factor in this political and cultural context, even if the thinking of the two curators was not directly related to the then political situation.

The US curators played a considerable role in deciding the ways in which the Korean culture should be presented to US audiences. Whether they intended to or not, America can be said to have intervened in the formation of the cultural identity of a fledgling nation-state of South Korea because it influenced the process in which Korean identity was being formed through material culture in the early stage of the South Korean nation-state.[42] This influence was significant in that Koreans would get to recognise their own cultural identity filtered through American intellectuals, while the US itself was yet in the course of making an image of national identity for South Korea that the US considered as adequate in the new order.

Thus, the Korean public as well as American audiences were exposed to Korean material culture through as US filter (Jang, 2016, pp. 460–1). Before those items that the American curators finally selected were sent to the US, NMK provided South Koreans with a chance to view the American-selected Korean national treasures by holding a special exhibition entitled *Korean National Treasures Which Will Be Exhibited in the US* in May 1957 (NMK, 1957).[43] In a sense, the Korean public as well as intellectuals got to see them through the filter of the US intellectuals[44] (Figure 2.3).

The first venue of the touring exhibition, *Masterpieces of Korean Art: An Exhibition under the Auspices of the Government of the Republic of Korea*, was in the National Gallery of Art in Washington, DC. The opening ceremony of the exhibition was held on 14 December 1957 and attracted 1,845 guests, including Walter S. Robertson (1953–1959 in office), Assistant Secretary of the State for Far Eastern Affairs; Earl Warren (1891–1974), Chief Justice of the Supreme Court; Garrison Norton (1900–1995), Assistant Secretary of the Navy; Yang Yu-Chan (1897–1975), the South Korean Ambassador to the US and various diplomatic delegates (Kim, 1991, p. 124). The presidents and their wives of the two countries were listed as honorary patrons of the exhibition.[45] This perfunctory designation

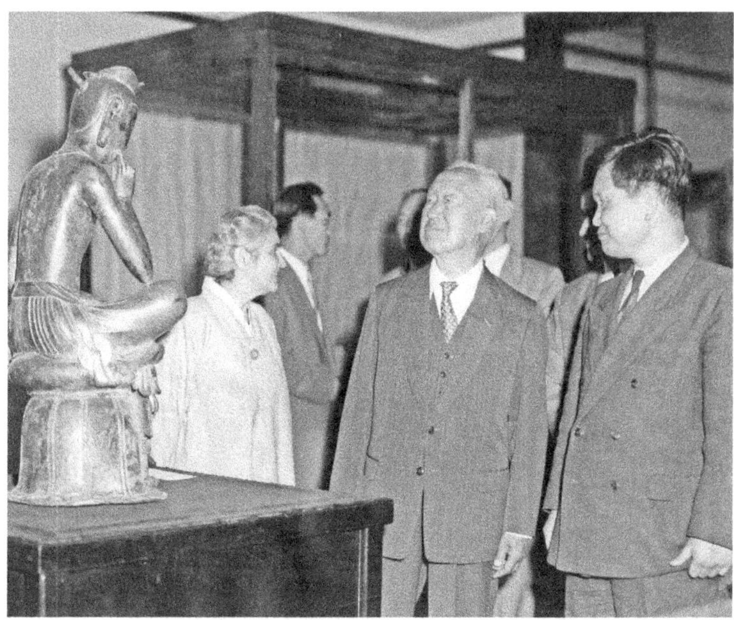

Figure 2.3 President Rhee Syngman at the special exhibition *Korean National Treasures Which Will be Exhibited in the US* in May 1957. With kind permission from the National Archives of Korea.

of high-ranking government officials as honorary patrons shows that this exhibition had deep diplomatic and political implications for the two countries' governments.

In the preface to the catalogue of the overseas exhibition in the US, Choi Kyu-nam (1898–1992), Minister of Education of the South Korean government, clearly expressed the political and diplomatic intention and meaning behind the exhibition. As he asserted in his preface, the South Korean government wanted the American government to understand that this exhibition was in return for US assistance in the Korean War. The Korean government was also eager to emphasise that South Korea was the most co-operative country in confronting the communist bloc. In other words, this exhibition can be said to have been intended as an extension of realpolitik between South Korea and the US.

Yang Yu-Chan, the ambassador to the US, reported the results of the opening of the exhibition to the President Rhee, saying, "I can frankly say that it seems there is a great deal of interest and publicity in this country. They have never seen or realised that such beautiful things existed in Korea."[46]

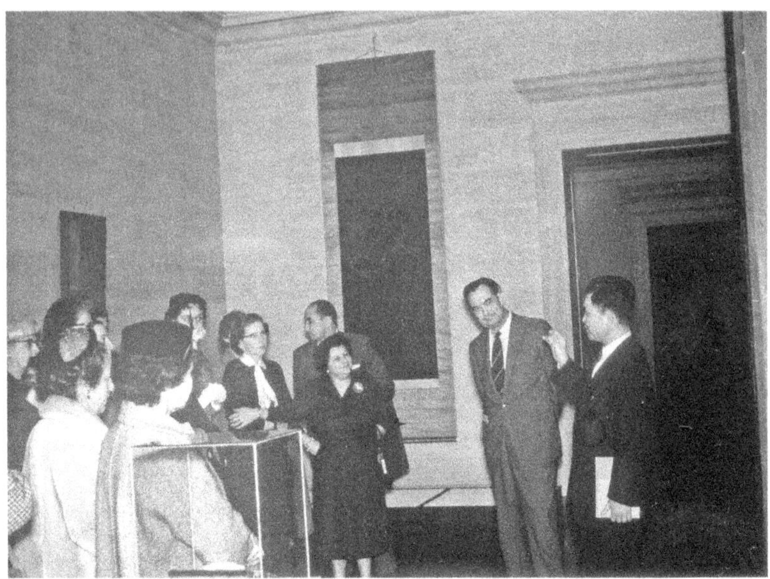

Figure 2.4 *Masterpieces of Korean Art* at the National Gallery of Art in December 1957. Copyright unknown.

Yang's comment shows that he was satisfied with the exhibition's diplomatic effect of publicizing Korean culture and Korea itself. Korea therefore was trying to achieve recognition of its national identity through material culture in the centre of the new world order presided over by the US. The Koreans' satisfaction with this recognition would lead to the firm position of the US on the Korean peninsula, both culturally and politically (Figure 2.4).

The American press also focused on individual and distinctive characteristics that distinguished Korean material culture from that of the neighbouring cultures, especially Chinese culture. One thing is clear: American intellectuals and journalists were eager to find unique and distinctive characteristics of Korean culture, even if they were able to point out Chinese influences in Korean culture. But more important was that, in the contemporary political and cultural context, they did not want to. The following report by the *New York Times* shows this tendency:

> What remains is sufficient to reveal that the art stubbornly maintained individual characteristics. These characteristics distinguish it from the more familiar Chinese and Japanese work with which the Occident

> has become increasingly acquainted since the end of World War Two. … The paintings, while relating to Chinese art in the bird and animal themes and such calligraphic examples as the traditional bamboo spray, nevertheless depart in organization and in various characteristics of drawing from any slavish eclecticism.[47]

This tone of the press on a culture of the Far East was not unfamiliar to Americans, because they had already experienced the same tone when they had seen the exhibition from Japan in 1953 (National Gallery of Art et al., 1953, pp. 7–10).[48] The same art critic reported on the Japanese exhibition for the *New York Times*:

> While debts to the art of China and to Buddhism are acknowledged, the art of Japan was nevertheless very much its own long before the later wood block prints captured the fancies of the Impressionists and their successors. This art has an amazing personality of its own.[49]

Thus, the American press was seeking new perspectives on cultures of the Far East. It seems that this trend had to do with the then international situation. It was clear that the US was trying to cultivate friendly countries in the Far East. Therefore, US recognition of each country's national identity through material culture can be said to have been essential and effective (Jang, 2016, pp. 464–6).

This first large-scale exhibition of Korean cultural objects, *Masterpieces of Korean Art*, attracted 167,731 visitors in eight American cities over 18 months from December 1957 to June 1959. Choi Sunu, director of NMK from 1974 to 1983, who was a courier for this exhibition, defined it as "the most grand overseas 'sacred festival' executed under the name of our nation," and said that it tried to "demonstrate our continuous achievements in art history that couldn't be second to any other nation and explain the unusual characteristics of our fine art." He further asserted that the "outcome of this project couldn't be achieved even by 200 diplomats and has a very important meaning both domestically and internationally."[50]

This overseas exhibition project was a significant success for the South Korean government as well as for NMK. This was because they both believed they had a great opportunity to teach Americans about the existence of a new nation, the Republic of Korea. Another important aspect was that politicians and museum curators in Korea got to know that the overseas exhibitions could be a very useful means to give publicity to the identity of Korea. Specifically, it was through this overseas exhibition in the US that they realised that cultural objects could be utilised for national interests if they could give some 'national' meanings and values to them.[51]

Nevertheless, there were almost no American experts on Korean art or on Korean history at that time. In most cases, curators for Japanese art took charge of the overseas tour exhibition. Director Kim even complained that they used Japanese terms regarding Korean ceramics (Kim, 1957, p. 302). Likewise, Korea had only a few academics in art history and archaeology. During Japanese colonial rule, the Japanese almost entirely monopolised those fields, and museums did not employ Koreans with only a few exceptions. NMK pushed forward several research projects, but it was not possible to construct a systematic understanding of material culture of Korea with such a short academic experience of it. South Korean curators thus just sought the interpretation of cultural objects in terms of a nationalist perspective. However, those efforts were a part of the process of searching for a cultural identity of a nation. It was in this way that Koreans began to learn a modern way of understanding and securing their cultural identity through material culture (Jang, 2016, pp. 464–6).

Notes

1 Military Government Annex to the 24th Corps Field Order No.35, 1 September 1945.
2 *Army and Navy Manual of Military Government and Civil Affairs*, 12 December 1943 (US Army FM27-5): "It is the policy of the United States, except where military necessity makes it impossible, to preserve all historical and cultural monuments and works, religious shrines and objects of art."
3 Military Government Annex 8 to Operations Instructions No.4, GHQ USAPP, 28 August 1945 (National Archives, RG 332, Box 64).
4 Subject: Arts, Monuments, and Religion: Preliminary Report, the Bureau of Education, USAMGIK, 3 October 1945 (National Archives, RG 332, Box 64).
5 Ibid.
6 Ibid.
7 Anon., "A History of the National Museum," in NMK, *Gwanbo* [National Museum Gazette], vol.1, February 1947, p. 1.
8 Ibid.
9 Ibid.
10 In an essay written in 1948, Kim criticised Japanese scholars for the Japanese exclusion of Koreans in the academic world. See Kim, "Amerika tongsin [News from America]," in *Hakpung*, April 1949. Cited in Kim, 1991, p. 267.
11 *The Dong-A Ilbo*, 4 December 1945.
12 "Director's foreword," in NMK, *Gwanbo*, vol.1, February 1947, p.i.
13 Ibid.
14 In his memoir, Arimitsu also stated that Kim must have been behind that decision. See Arimitsu, 1985b, pp. 112–13.
15 Kim Chewon, "Gyeongju gobun balgul ui bogo [A Report of the Excavation in Gyeongju]," *The Seoul Shinmun*, 7 July 1946.
16 NMK, *Gwanbo*, vol.1, 1947, pp. 5–6. During colonial rule, the national language was Japanese while Korean was a local dialect. In 1940, the colonial

authorities shut down all Korean language newspapers save the Government-General organ, *Mail sinbo* (Robinson, 1990, p. 318). This action was conceived as a bitter humiliation by most Koreans.

17 Ibid.

18 Ibid.

19 *The Dong-A Ilbo*, 11 May 1946; *The Dong-A Ilbo*, 11 March 1947.

20 In his memoirs, Kim (1992, p. 326) recollected, "I could not understand why we Koreans worship Dangun as our progenitor and adopt an endemic calendar system, arguing our history is 5,000 years long." From 1948 to 1961, the South Korean government officially used its own calendar system, called Dan-gi, counting from 2333 BCE (the year 1948, when the South Korean government was established, equates to the Dan-gi year 4281). The notion of a 5,000-year-long history of Korea is directly related to this calendar, and was used as a part of the title of the second overseas special exhibition of NMK from 1976 to 1984.

21 Kim Chewon, "Wigi ui gukbo geonchuk [National treasure Architecture in Crisis]" *The Seoul Shinmun*, 15 July 1947.

22 For example, there was no word related to ethnic nation in the museum mission of NMK, which was established in the first part of the 1950s. This museum mission will be discussed later in this chapter.

23 See Eckert, 1990c, pp. 327–9. He says, South Korean society had already been divided in ideology during the colonial period. USAMGIK openly declared freedom of thought in South Korea when they advanced to South Korea in 1945, but the reality was by far more difficult than they thought. Communists and leftists gradually came into conflict with USAMGIK as well as with rightist factions. Eventually, USAMGIK illegalised the Korean Communist Party in 1946.

24 *Jayu shinmun*, 8 May 1946.

25 Every visit by important figures was recorded in *Gwanbo* published between 1945 and 1949.

26 After resigning from the foundation in 1961, in 1962 Fahs was appointed Minister-Councelor of Cultural and Public Affairs at the US Embassy in Tokyo. See "Biographical/Historical Note," *Charles Berton Fahs Papers (FA099)*, Rockefeller Archive Center. Available at https://dimes.rockarch.org/FA099/bio-hist. Accessed 15 December 2019. This suggests a close cooperation between the US government and US-based foundations.

27 Salmony had worked for the Asian Art Museum of Cologne, and fled to the US to avoid Nazi persecution. See Kim, 1991, pp. 64–6.

28 The excavation of the Houchong tomb in 1946 was reported in *Artibus Asiae* by Kim. See Kim Chewon, "Two Old Sila Tombs," *Artibus Asiae*, vol.10, no.3, 1947, pp. 169–92.

29 This programme was made possible by the Smith-Mundt Act (the US Information and Educational Exchange Act of 1948, Public Law 80-402). See Heo Eun, *Miguk ui hegemoni wa hanguk minjokjuui* [The US Hegemony and Korean Ethnic Nationalism], Seoul: Institute of Ethnic National Culture Research, Korea University, 2008, p. 93 & p. 214. Salmony was scheduled to deliver 14 lectures on East Asian art and archaeology over three months, but did just one because of the outbreak of the Korean War on 25 June 1950. See Kim, 1991, p. 65.

30 Griffing, who was keen to hold the exhibition in Hawaii, became a key person to revive the discussion after the Korean War. His academy finally could hold *Masterpieces of Korean Art* in 1959.

31 They included not only Korean artefacts but also Chinese artefacts, such as a Han China lacquerware with paintings excavated in Korea, which actually drew more attention from American academics (Kim, 1992, pp. 100–10).

32 Lee Hong-jik, acting director of NMK during Kim's stay in the US, stated that Director Kim's visit to the US was worthy of special mention in that he secured a way to accessing substantial financial support for NMK's future projects from the Rockefeller Foundation in the future. See NMK, *Gwanbo*, vol.6, March 1949, p. 19.

33 NMK, *Gwanbo*, vol.7, September 1949, p. 5.

34 Ibid., p. 6.

35 The North Korean press, even in terms of the excavation of Houchong tomb in 1946, severely criticised the US and their Korean collaborators for "looting" Korean cultural objects. See Knez, 'Special Contribution,' in Kim, 1991, p. 104. See also Knez, 1997, pp. 27–8.

36 On 9 July 1951, Rhee ordered the evacuation of NMK's collection to Hawaii. See NMK, *Gungnip jungang bangmulgwan yuksipnyeon* [60 Years of the National Museum of Korea], Seoul: 2006, p. 48.

37 NMK, "*Gungnip bangmulgwan hyeonhwang josa bogoseo* [National Museum Business Report]," February 1955.

38 Ibid.

39 NMK, *Gwanbo*, vol.1, July 1947, p.i.

40 This overseas exhibition, which opened on 14 December, 1957 at the National Gallery of Art, toured seven more cities, New York (The Metropolitan Museum of Art), Boston (Museum of Fine Arts), Seattle (Seattle Art Museum), Minneapolis (The Minneapolis Institute of Art), San Francisco (California Palace of the Legion of Honor), Los Angeles (Los Angeles County Museum) and Honolulu (Honolulu Academy of Arts), until 7 June 1959, attracting 167,731 people in total. The exhibition contained 193 objects including 18 metalcrafts, 24 sculptures, 35 paintings, 109 porcelains and 7 bricks. See Ministry of Education, 1960, pp. 21–31 and Jang, 2015, p. 129.

41 Memo, From P-Walter K. Schwinn, 14 August 1951, Subject: U.S. Information and Educational Exchange Programs in the Present Situation, p. 2. Cited in Heo, 2008, p. 328.

42 In 1960, many artefacts displayed in this exhibition were designated as "national treasures" by the government after returning from the touring exhibition.

43 This exhibition, which attracted an audience of 51,092 from 10 May to 21 May, was demanded by members of the National Assembly in the course of the examination of the motion by the government in May 1955. They contended that South Koreans should view the exhibition before it went overseas, criticizing the fact that NMK had not yet opened permanent galleries before that time.

44 In terms of this overseas exhibition, NMK published its first catalogue, titled *Gukbo dogam* [An Illustrated Guide to National Treasures], to include those 193 items which will be exhibited in the US in December 1957.

45 The Honourable Dwight D. Eisenhower, President of the United States of America, and Mrs. Eisenhower, His Excellency Syngman Rhee, President of the Republic of Korea, and Mrs. Rhee. See National Gallery of Art et al., *Masterpieces of Korean Art*, 1957, p. 7.

46 A letter from Ambassador Yang to President Rhee, 19 December 1957 (MOFAS Diplomatic Archives 773.1US, O-0010, 59)

47 Devree, Howard (1958) "Art: 300 Korean Works, Sculpture, Painting, Ceramics and Gold Objects Shown at the Metropolitan," *New York Times*, 7 February 1958.

48 In 1953, five US museums including the National Gallery of Art held the touring exhibition, *Japanese Painting and Sculpture*.

49 Devree, Howard (1953) "Treasures of Japan, Sheer Beauty Dominates Metropolitan Show," *New York Times*, 29 February 1953.

50 Choi, Sunu (1957) "Wosington ui gomisuljeon [Ancient Arts Exhibition in Washington]," *The Seoul Shinmun*, 13 December 1957.

51 This touring exhibition in the US drew some attention from several Western European countries, such as the United Kingdom and West Germany. Since opening in London on 23 March 1961, this exhibition toured four more Western European cities, The Hague, Paris, Frankfurt and Vienna, until 1 July 1962, attracting 53,246 people in total. See Jang, 2015, pp. 131–3 and Horlyck & Priewe, 2018, pp. 92–7.

3 Ethnic nationalism and museum narrative

After the Korean War, anti-communist sentiment permeated South Korean society. The resulting division of the peninsula challenged the notion of a single ethnic nation, because this could imply compromise or collaboration with the communist North. Scholars point out that President Rhee Syngman (in office from 1948 to 1960) took the lead in spreading this sentiment, and wanted fully to utilise it for his long-term seizure of power (Cho, 2010, pp. 228–36).[1] In this view, ethnic nationalism in South Korea was never dynamic in the late 1950s, although Rhee partly utilised his career and fame as a fighter for independence (Lee, 2013, p. 233).[2]

However, student demonstrations against his dictatorship and his ruling party's rigged election in March 1960 led to his resignation in April 1960. Chang Myeon's (1899–1966) regime followed, and it had to meet South Koreans' expectations for democracy and economic development; however, it was not competent in dealing with the outpouring of expectations (Lee, 2013, pp. 274–84; Cho, 2007, pp. 31–2). Park Chung Hee's regime took an interest in the potential of the notion of an ethnic nation. Park, who seized power after a military coup on 16 May 1961, pushed forward ethnic awareness as another means of mobilising South Koreans for the "reconstruction of the country," although he continued to resort to anti-communism as before (Cho, 2010, p. 297).[3] Convincing them that "ethnic community" was synonymous with "country," and asking the people for sacrifice made for the good of the ethnic community, Park began to extract the potential to develop the economy of the country and secure his political interests.

This regime, which would hold power for 18 years until Park was assassinated by his right-hand man in October 1979, put forward the notion of an ethnic nation for contributing to the solidarity of the people, and thus supporting his political ambitions (Jeon, 1998, pp. 1–3; Seo, 2007, pp. 192–212; Cho, 2010, pp. 62–3; Lee, 2013, p. 301). Park's regime took an interest in the discovery and display of the Korean ethnic culture, including material culture (Oh, 1998, pp. 121–52; Jeon, 1998, pp. 178–83; Lee, 2002, pp. 54–7; Park, 2010, p. 70).

Park Chung Hee and the rhetoric of ethnic nationalism

Calling his military coup a revolution, Park Chung Hee (1917–1979) focused on the opposition to communism, the construction of an independent national economy and the recovery of the righteous spirit of the ethnic nation. The coup was followed by the prohibition of all political activities and the replacement of the National Assembly with an ultra-constitutional Supreme Council for National Reconstruction, which Park chaired and the military managed. The military also took over the civil service, and officers became ministers.

On 7 July 1961, the minister of the Department of Education issued directions to officials of the local governments for the fulfilment of the culture and education policy of the new government. This policy had four main goals: the defeat of communist intervention or invasion, reform in humanity, eradication of poverty and innovation in culture. By criticising the "cultural phenomenon of idleness and decadence," the government showed it understood education and culture as a medium for "cultivating people who could find their life purpose in the service for the ethnic nation and the country." Interestingly, the ultimate goal of the innovation of culture was described as "the construction of ethnic national culture."[4]

On 1 January 1962, in a New Year's address, Park requested that all efforts and sincerity of the entire nation be fully mobilised for achieving the goals of the first year of the his five-year plan for economic development, emphasising that an ethnic nation was an eternal creature.[5] Through his speeches and policies in this early phase, Park repeatedly reminded South Koreans of their common destiny, using the evocative vocabulary "brethren," "forefather" and "fatherland." Indeed, the first word in his inaugural address as the fifth president of the Republic of Korea in December 1963 was "Dangun," the sacred progenitor.[6] He also added that "the solidarity of the ethnic nation without the non-cooperation or factional strife is the only way to the modernisation of the fatherland." It can be said that the notion of an ethnic nation was intended as a magical idea under which all Koreans should unite, whether or not they agreed with Park's policy. Park's address revealed his attempt to unite the South Korean people with the concept of the ethnic nation and, in doing so, facilitated his political ambition.

By contrast, Park and his military government strived to produce a vision of economic development, and to this end they introduced a series of reforms. As Cho points out, the government's strong point was its dynamic drive, as shown in its military operations; however, the government's emphasis was on the achievement of goals rather than democratic debate (Cho, 2007, pp. 44–5). The new government was no less diligent in the reform of cultural heritage policy, establishing the Office of Cultural Properties in October 1961 and enacting the Cultural Properties Preservation Act in January 1962. It also repaired two key national treasures, the Great South Gate in Seoul and Seokguram Grotto in Gyeongju, between July and October 1961. These various actions taken by the government led to some positive media responses and the press re-emphasised the responsibility of the government to preserve cultural objects.[7]

Park's regime set about improving the infrastructure of the ethnic national culture as a matter of urgency for the sake of cultural innovation. However, the regime was more interested in the instrumental function of culture than in the actual culture itself. It was also in this context that the military government began to pay attention to the discourse on ethnic national culture for propelling ethnic nationalism (Oh, 1998, p. 123). Park began to realise the political implications of ethnic culture during the interim period before he was elected president. In April 1962, Park's speech at the "Silla Cultural Festival," held at Gyeongju, which was the capital of the Silla dynasty, showed how Park's nationalism coated communal sensibility with national heritage.[8]

From Park's viewpoint, the cultural heritage were enough concrete evidence to show the possibilities of reconstruction, innovation in and creation of the Korean ethnic nation. Furthermore, he found that culture could be a means to mobilise the nationwide cooperation of the populace. Thus, Park and his government added another meaning to the expression of ethnic national culture: that is, a norm of solidarity which the entire nation should observe. This explains why he repeatedly emphasised the creation and innovation of ethnic national culture from his early days in power.

"Ethnic national culture" arrives at the museum

This discourse on ethnic national culture began to influence NMK in the form of guidelines from the government. Status reports written up by NMK for annual audits shows these influences. A status report from the year 1962 did not include the expression "ethnic national culture." Instead, it specified detailed tasks such as the publication of the museum gazette and investigations of ancient tombs which suffered grave robberies. Along with the budget allocated to those tasks. It also adopted a yearly planner in order to show that each task of the year would be executed in due course.[9] This change reflected the fact that the military government put emphasis on administrative effectiveness. Indeed, those military personnel who were trained in military administration during the 1950s comprised one of few groups with modern sensibilities in South Korea (Cho, 2007, pp. 44–5). The military government demanded an effective administration throughout government by reinforcing performance management. This demand of NMK for effectiveness was described as being for its ultimate goal: the inheritance and development of ethnic national culture.

The 1963 NMK status report stated that cultural innovation was a policy goal of the Ministry of Education, and the report went on to define two further objectives. The first was to inherit and develop ethnic national culture, and by doing so to promote public education through the effective management of cultural institutions. The second was to promote the creation of a new ethnic national culture by discovering and displaying that ethnic national culture.[10] Like the precedent of 1962, each task and its detailed project were specified along with a budget allocation. All of these changes meant that all the expenditure by national cultural institutions should be transparent and explained through an understanding of ethnic national culture.

This government-led nationalist drive ultimately intended that museum collections be considered "ethnic national cultural objects."[11] This drive led to a gradual increase in the budget of NMK. However, the budget increase between 1962 and 1963 was mainly due to the rise in wages of the staff, approved following the coup. Although the government sought political utilisation of the discourse on ethnic national culture, it could never afford to invest enough in the culture field when industrialisation began in the country. Before 1972, there was no practical increase in the number of the staff, either. The government focused on the construction and spread of the discourse rather than practical investment in institutions related to ethnic national culture (Table 3.1).

Beginning in 1967, the government began to increase the budget of the national museum.[12] The success of the first five-year-long economic development plan (1962 to 1966) gave the government a chance to drastically increase investment in the cultural sector. Park was willing to utilise the ethnic national culture agenda in order to win his second presidential election in May 1967. He also grew confident that this utilisation of ethnic national culture could play a practical role in mobilising the people for the economic development and industrialisation of Korea.

In this context, the government began to pay attention to cultural objects. Its focus was on both the restoration of popular cultural relics and expansion of the museum facilities. Both actions were expected to realise the government's will to promote ethnic national culture. At the ground-breaking ceremony of a new building for NMK at Gyeongbokgung Palace in Seoul in November 1966, President Park remarked on his expectations of the national museum by stating, "I hope the General Cultural Centre project, including this museum, will make a substantial contribution to

Table 3.1 Manpower and budget of NMK, 1958 to 1973

Year	*1958*	*1959*	*1960*	*1961*	*1962*	*1963*	*1964*	*1965*
Manpower	*35*	*?*	*45*	*46*	*44*	*44*	*44*	*?*
Budget (unit: 1,000 won)	2,269	3,445	6,636	6,905	7,769	8,690	8,304	9,663
GNP per capita of South Korea (USD)	80	81	79	82	87	100	103	105
Year	*1966*	*1967*	*1968*	*1969*	*1970*	*1971*	*1972*	*1973*
Manpower	*47*	*47*	*47*	*51*	*51*	*51*	*72*	*115*
Budget (unit: 1,000 won)	12,004	18,429	23,776	81,130	120,459	116,134	348,836	348,883
GNP per capita of South Korea (USD)	125	142	169	210	253	289	319	396

* Compiled from the National Museum of Korea, *Gungnip jungang bangmulgwan yuksipnyeon* [60 Years of the National Museum of Korea], Seoul, 2006, p. 672, and Ministry of Culture and Information, *Munhwagongbo samsipnyeon* [30 Years of Culture and Information], Seoul, 1979, pp. 323–4.

the construction of the rich and powerful fatherland and this rich ethnic nation."[13] His address showed that he considered the national museum as a concrete medium to persuade the entire nation that all of them were members of one ethnic nation. At this ceremony, his emphasis was on the development of the nation rather than the culture itself.

On 24 July 1968, the government established the Ministry of Culture and Information in order to integrate its public information function with affairs related to culture; this had formerly been under the supervision of the Ministry of Education (Ministry of Culture and Information, 1979, p. 224). As Kim Seong-jin, the Minister of Culture and Information from 1975 to 1979, said, this reorganisation was so that "both the policy of culture and government PR could improve mutually in the context of enhancement of national independence and play a role as the spiritual mainstay for the development of the country" (Ministry of Culture and Information, 1979, p. 224). It was from this point on that NMK and the Office of Cultural Properties under the ministry gradually began to expand.

The government pushed forward a series of construction projects for local branch museums in Buyeo, Gongju and Gyeongju from 1966 to 1975. These projects made it possible for NMK to refurbish all of the facilities that it had inherited from GGM. These new museum buildings were intended to be the visualisation of governmental policy for enhancing community spirit through ethnic national culture. As a result, NMK had a new building in 1972, and branch museums in Buyeo and Gyeongju museums had new buildings in 1971 and 1975, respectively. The Gongju branch museum secured its new building in 1973 thanks to the discovery of a royal tomb in 1971, which produced a large quantity of artefacts. It is worth noting that local branch museums were also instrumental in developing Gyeongju and Buyeo, capitals of ancient kingdoms, as tourist attractions. The expense of the construction of local museums in Gyeongju and Buyeo was paid for from the special account for economic development, not the general accounts of the government. This helps to explain the relationship between political and economic investment in museum structures.

Discourse on ethnic national culture and the evolving narrative of NMK

The discourse on ethnic national culture as a political slogan began to influence the interpretation and narratives of Korean material culture. Park's remarks at the ground-breaking ceremony of NMK in 1966 are noteworthy:

> We inherited the excellent, brilliant and indigenous cultural heritage from our forefathers throughout its 5,000-year-long history.

> This cultural heritage is the fruit of the spirit and soul of our ethnic nation. The proper preservation and transmission of the heritage is our obligation that the entire nation should take on any ordeal and disorder.[14]

As shown above, Park declared that Korean cultural heritage was excellent and creative. It was a convincing guideline that NMK was encouraged to follow in understanding Korean culture. It also meant that NMK considered it a supreme task to find excellence in ethnic national culture through material culture. This recognition had already germinated within the independence movement from the colonial rule period, and was related to a new wave of independent interpretation of Korean history after liberation. However, his remark was meaningful in that South Korea's paramount leader considered ethnic national culture as a power for the development of the country, and in that he argued as fact the excellence and creativity of the culture, which had not been fully proved.

Interestingly, Park's remark had the same resonance with Korean academics, who were striving to criticise and overcome the view of Korean history set out by Japanese scholars during colonial rule. As already discussed, Japanese scholars had tried to justify colonial rule through their research. They generally argued that Korean society had been stagnant throughout all ages, and had been dependent on Chinese culture. For example, Japanese archaeologists argued that there had been no Bronze Age in Korea (Kim, 1985, pp. 61–2), thereby excluding Korea from prehistoric human development.

Their argument that Korean history was riddled with toadyism and retrogression deeply influenced the Korean public as well as its intellectuals. Park remarked that "retreat, crudity and stagnation have marked out our 5,000 years of history" (Park, 1963, pp. 165–7). Even though his rhetoric, in a sense, reflected his political ambition to be considered as a leader who could get rid of all the evils inherited from the past, it was also clear that he was influenced by the Japanese view of Korean history (Choi, 2012, p. 187).[15] Furthermore, his understanding also reflected the Korean public's prevalent view. The systematic criticism of this view started within the academic circles of Korean history in the beginning of the 1960s. Defining the Japanese view as colonial view of history, Lee (1961, pp. 1–10) set out to challenge the Japanese discourse on Korean society's toadyism, stagnation and factionalism. Korean academics strove to prove the self-sustainable development of Korean culture, and to find the creativity of the Korean culture as well as its differences from Chinese culture.

They recognised that the prehistoric age and Joseon Period were the main targets of Japanese distortion. First, the culture of the Joseon dynasty was derided, and the main reason was explained as because of its stagnation and lack of creativity caused by toadyism toward China. This alleged cultural decline was so serious that the Japanese could justify annexation of Korea (Sekino, 1932, pp. 3–7). Korean academics therefore realised that it was an urgent issue to criticise this distorted view of the dynasty. The Japanese scholars put little emphasis on the prehistoric age of Korea. They tended to argue that Korean history actually started from the establishment of a Chinese commandery, called Nangnang, in 108 BCE. In this regard, they denied the universal prehistoric development process in the Korean peninsula before the establishment of the commandery. These arguments were a main target of Korean academics' criticism.

From the time that it was established, NMK, the only centre for studying Korean material culture, strove to conduct research and set up exhibition projects to aid in criticising these Japanese arguments. The increase in budget in NMK in the late 1960s made this possible. The archaeological projects of NMK focused on proving the universal development process of civilisation in the prehistoric age of Korea. While the excavations during the 1950s were for providing training for archaeological skills, and were lacking a systematic academic purpose, these projects had the clear objectives of critiquing the argument that Korea had always benefited from the Chinese culture from the prehistoric age onwards, and that there had been no distinct development of the Bronze Age found in the Korean peninsula (Kim, 1985, pp. 61–2).

NMK investigated many dolmen relics throughout the country from 1962 to 1967, and excavated dwelling relics of the Bronze Age from 1967 to 1969, which aided in proving the existence of the Bronze Age in Korea (NMK, 2006, pp. 109–18). In addition, NMK published a collection catalogue in 1968 that detailed the Bronze Age artefacts collected since the liberation.[16] From 1969 to 1971 NMK also investigated a shell mound on the coast of Busan in order to study the neolithic culture in Korean peninsula. In addition, the excavation of the shell mounds around the southern coast of Korea from 1965 to 1970 investigated the cultural and historical aspects of the early state formation stage. Indeed, NMK's excavations of relics of the prehistoric age were, literally, for studying the origin of Korean ethnic national culture, as shown in the definition of the tasks of NMK of the year 1970. These activities of NMK were described as for establishing ethnic national subjectivity.[17]

By contrast, exhibitions of NMK in the 1960s concentrated on shedding new light on the culture of the Joseon dynasty (1392–1910), especially during the latter part (17th–19th centuries) of the dynasty.[18] NMK was trying to rehabilitate the cultural status of the dynasty. The exhibitions in this period covered various fields such as porcelain, furniture, ornaments, lanterns and costumes of the Joseon dynasty, and especially paintings, giving a separate introduction to each detailed genre of painting, that is, portraits, genre paintings and landscapes (NMK, 2006, pp. 78–81). These exhibitions were clearly meant to critique the arguments of Japanese scholars as well as to affirm the meaning and worth of the culture of the Joseon dynasty. In another sense, these exhibitions argued that even during the Joseon dynasty, Korea had enough cultural capacity to maintain its independence, and should not have been colonised by Japan.

NMK took the lead in the study of Korean material culture and also played an essential role in organising the Korean Archaeological Society in 1967 and the Art History Association of Korea in 1968. These organisations would play an important role in securing a concrete platform for an independent discourse of Korean material culture, as well as in cultivating new academics in those fields.

The October revitalisation and promotion of ethnic national culture

Park managed to amend the constitution in order to make his third term possible, and he succeeded in being elected again in April 1971; however, the election was a tight race, and corrupt. On 6 December 1971, he declared a state of national emergency. He dissolved the National Assembly on 17 October 1972 and replaced it with the Emergency Council for National Affairs, which meant that he wanted to shut down the legislative body. Park pushed forward with amending the Constitution in the name of constructing a strong government for unification. Through the national referendum under emergency martial law, the so-called Revitalisation Constitution was approved and promulgated on 27 December 1972, portending the most systematic dictatorship in the modern political history of Korea (Cumings, 2005, p. 363; Kim, 1999, p. 234; Brazinsky, 2007, p. 160). The National Council for Unification, organised by this constitution, had the right to elect the president, and one-third of the National Assembly members of the candidates were recommended by the president. The president automatically became the chairman of the council and effectively controlled the council. On 23 December 1972, Park was again elected as the president with an indirect election by the council. This constitution paved the way for Park's life-long seizure of power and dictatorship, incapacitating the National Assembly (Cho, 2007, pp. 142–50).

The term "*Yusin*," or revitalisation, originated from the Meiji Restoration (1868) of the empire of Japan. This concept was intended as synonymous with the thorough reform for so-called ethnic national restoration, suggesting that Park would strongly push forward ethnic nationalist policies for his political ambition. This slogan of ethnic national restoration had already appeared in the early 1960s and was commonplace in the 1970s. A representative example of this is the announcement of the Charter of National Education on 5 December 1968, which appeared on the first page of every textbook from that time forwards.

The notion of ethnic nation became increasingly important as an absolute cause for which the entire nation should serve. Under this strong wave of ethnic nationalism, the government increased the investments in the ethnic national culture and art sectors. At the inaugural address for his third term, in July 1971, Park remarked:

> Being certain that the talent of this wise ethnic nation will develop, I will inherit and develop the brilliant tradition and culture [inherited] from our forebears, and have special interest in the restoration of the ethnic national culture and provide full support for it by promoting art, culture and scholarship.[19]

The government promulgated the Culture and Art Promotion Act in August 1972 and, in the same year, set up a comprehensive plan for the development of Gyeongju as an ancient capital over a 10-year period, according to Park's direction.

Park's emphasis on art and culture also was a result of the socio-economic changes in South Korea. Economic growth since the 1960s had created a new demand for cultural consumption from the early 1970s (Ministry of Culture and Information, 1979, p. 226). Park needed to absorb and control this demand. The government's solution was the creation of new ethnic national culture, based on the notion of the ethnic nation. Accordingly, the government's concept of culture had to be necessarily connected to the ethnic nation or the country, not to the individual or civilian society. This meant that ethnic culture as described by the government was intended to be not only the culture itself but also a code of conduct which the government expected from the nation. In this context, it was natural to put an emphasis on cultural objects or material culture which could easily arouse the notion of community.

At his fourth inaugural address, in December 1972, Park reasserted his will to "employ policy for revitalising culture and art by developing our genuine traditional culture more creatively, so that the flower of ethnic national culture could be in full bloom." Therefore, the government promulgated the Five Year Long Plan for Revitalising Culture and Art (1974–1978). On 20 October 1973, representative Korean artists and writers adopted the Declaration for Revitalising Culture and Art, emphasising that "we keenly realise the mission of creating a new culture at a turning point in revitalising the ethnic nation."[20]

For the next five years, the government invested about 485 billion *won* in total for the plan. More than 70 per cent of the budget was spent on the cultural heritage sector, as shown in Table 3.2 (Ministry of Culture and Information, 1979, pp. 228–9). This cultural heritage sector, which was described as being for the "establishment of the nationalist view of history," was categorised into detailed fields, such as cultural objects, national (Korean) studies and traditional arts and crafts. Out of these three fields, the cultural objects field had been allocated an overwhelming proportion of the budget, as Table 3.2 shows.

In terms of Park's utilisation of cultural heritage for his politics, it is very telling that President Park visited NMK and viewed a special exhibition entitled *Masterpieces of 500 Years of Korean Painting* on 22 November 1972, when the Revitalisation Constitution was passed by national referendum. A day later, a photograph of Park viewing the exhibition was published on the first page of a major newspaper.[21] He was doing the right thing for the ethnic nation from his perspective.

Reopening of NMK in 1972

As discussed earlier in this chapter, Park's interest in the cultural heritage sector was realised through the physical elements of museums: the new buildings of NMK in Seoul and the local branch museums. In 1969, NMK absorbed the Deoksugung Museum of Art (the former Yi Royal Household Museum), representing a decisive desire to upgrade its collection. This merger gave NMK a landmark chance to secure 12,481 artefacts, including artworks of a high standard. Because of this, the collection of the Deoksugung Museum of Art had a chance of appearing on the stage of ethnic national culture.

After six years of construction, NMK was reopened in the new building situated at Gyeongbokgung Palace, in Seoul on 25 August 1972, with President Park and his wife attending the opening ceremony. This new building, the galleries of which were twice the size of those of the former, was equipped with 10 galleries, which chronologically displayed the material culture of each dynasty, like the Three Kingdoms, the Goryeo and the Joseon, as well as the prehistoric period.[22] New permanent exhibitions showed a couple of remarkable changes, reflecting the accumulation of both NMK and South Korean academics since 1945. In addition, these changes were closely related to the ultimate goal of discovering the independence and uniqueness of Korean culture since the prehistoric age. This drive was triggered not only by the government but also by scholars (Figure 3.1). Overcoming the colonial view of Korean history was the almost common task of South Korean academics.

Table 3.2 Government budget invested in culture and the art field during the 5-year-plan period, 1974 to 1978 (Unit: 1 million won)

	Total	*Proportion*	*1974*	*1975*	*1976*	*1977*	*1978*
Total	48,542.4	100.0%	4,239.0	4,757.9	5,464.2	12,322.0	21,759.3
1. Construction of basic foundation	2,881.8	6.0%	173.4	455.2	744.3	1,009.8	499.1
2. Cultural heritage	34,079.7	70.2%	2,206.6	2,719.8	3001.0	8,818.0	17.334.3
-National studies	1,603.0	3.3%	632.0	137.4	119.6	366.3	348.0
-Traditional arts	1,844.5	3.8%	187.8	94.3	158.3	311.8	1,092.3
-Cultural objects	30,631.9	63.1%	1,386.8	2,488.1	2,723.1	8,139.9	15,894.0
3. Arts	5,929.8	12.2%	1,200.1	825.1	858.4	1,347.4	1,698.8
4. Pop culture	4,300.7	8.9%	544.1	535.3	637.4	1,103.3	1,480.6
5. Others	1,350.4	2.7%	114.8	222.5	223.1	43.5	746.5

Source: Ministry of Culture and Information, 1979, p. 228.

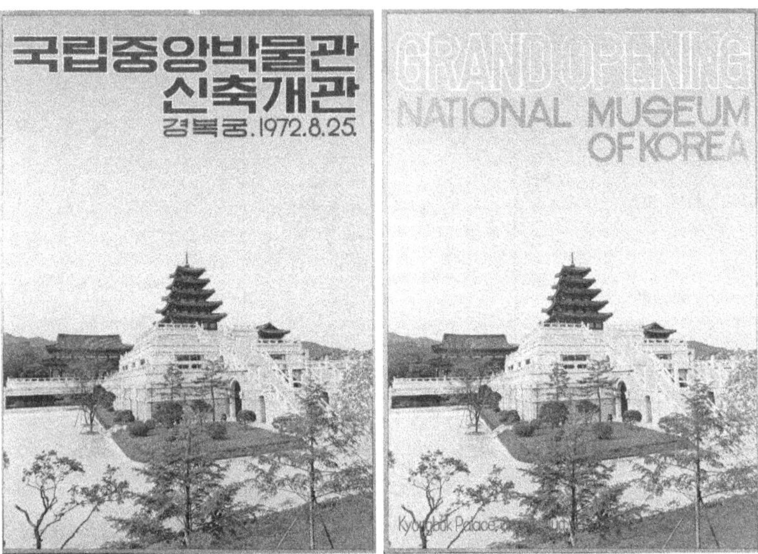

Figure 3.1 Posters in commemoration of the reopening of the National Museum of Korea in Gyeongbokgung Palace in August 1972. With kind permission from NMK.

In this regard, the gallery for the prehistoric age was greatly strengthened in comparison with its former building, and its exhibits tried to explain to visitors that Korea had experienced a universal development process of civilisation through periods such as the Neolithic Age, Bronze Age and Iron Age.[23] The argument that there had been no Bronze Age in the Korean peninsula was considered a colonial view, and so it was vital that it be denied through material evidence. It was for this reason that NMK published a catalogue, "Selected Bronze Objects of the Early Metal Period," as early as 1968. However, the concept of the early metal period supposed the coexistence of the Bronze Age and the Iron Age, which was not all that different from the Japanese argument. NMK hesitated to use the term Bronze Age. However, when opening new galleries in 1972, NMK did say "Bronze Age" in its catalogue (NMK, 1972, pp. 11–12). In this regard, it is very suggestive that NMK, in October 1973, held a special exhibition, *Korean Bronze Artefacts in Prehistoric Age* to introduce the bronze artefacts excavated in Korea.[24]

The Japanese argument about the prehistoric age was actually supported by the existence of Nangnang on the grounds that it was this Nangnang culture, a part of Chinese culture, which first transmitted civilisation to the Korean peninsula.[25] This argument was effective in explaining that

Korean culture was, from the start, subordinate to Chinese culture. Yet Korean scholars were reluctant to accept this argument, and strived to find evidence against it. NMK took the decision to exclude the display of Nangnang culture from this new building. Even though space was secured on January 1974 for displaying the culture of Nangnang at the East Asian gallery. This culture was to be considered as a foreign culture introduced to Korea from the Chinese proper, and not as part of the origin of Korean ancient culture. This marked a change.

It was at this time that the first catalogue guide for domestic visitors was published (NMK, 1972). This 154-page book included photos of artefacts in chronological order, an introduction to Korean history and art and a floor map of the galleries. It provided explanations written in three languages: Korean, English and Japanese. Interestingly, this book introduced photos of artefacts from Nangnang between the prehistoric age and the Three Kingdoms Period, despite the exclusion of Nangnang's artefacts from the permanent gallery. This discrepancy showed both NMK's attitude towards Nangnang culture and its dilemma, namely its difficulty in dealing with the culture in a way which could support the colonial view of Korean history. Above all, the description in the catalogue still maintained a negative view of the culture of the Joseon dynasty, stating that "worldly oriented Confucianism dominated intellectual society, leaving little room for free thinking creative artists," even though it emphasised two exceptions, painting and ceramics (NMK, 1972, pp. 128, 138 and 149). Actually, this expression derived from the same remark written in the English version of the catalogue published in 1964 and did not reflect the new understanding of Korean academics, including NMK's curators. It can be said that this delay also reflected lack of confidence in the dynasty's cultural capacity, despite their continuous efforts so far.[26]

In April 1973, NMK held a large-scale special exhibition entitled *2000 Years of Korean Art*. For this ambitious exhibition, designed to make a comprehensive survey of Korean cultural objects, NMK displayed more than 600 items, 60 per cent of which were on loan from private collectors, public and private museums and Buddhist temples. This two-month-long exhibition, which attracted 235,242 people – including 40,000 foreigners – was a great success, and contributed to demonstrating that the existence of an ethnic nation could be proved through its material culture, sublimating artefacts into symbols of the ethnic nation.

In its status report of 1974, NMK reported that this exhibition enhanced the genuine value of ethnic national culture at home and abroad.[27] It reminded government officials and museum curators that the exhibition would be effective in educating the value of the ethnic nation or the ethnic national cultural objects and in internalising their value in the public consciousness. This exhibition convinced curators of the meaning and usefulness of ethnic nationalist interpretation of material culture.

The permanent exhibition in the new building in 1972 and the special exhibition were the outcome of the efforts for independent authorship that had been, in part, propelled by Park's ethnic nationalist policies. These exhibitions were also for critiquing the colonial view of Korean history and reconstructing the cultural identity of the Korean ethnic nation. A member of the curatorial staff member set out his mission:

> The crime for which the Japanese can never be forgiven is to try to obliterate Koreans' past ethnic culture. They attempted to make Korean nationals the subjects of their empire by demolishing and distorting our history, culture and tradition. … We have to clean up the remnants that they left behind, correct their distorted history and revive our forgotten traditional culture. For the last 30 years we have been able to newly acquire numerous cultural heritage objects and secure vivid materials of ancient history by excavating ancient relics, including prehistoric ones. On the basis of these resources, we should reconstruct our distorted ancient history and find Korean traditional beauty. We need to do our best to make our Korean nationals understand our traditional culture, which has been isolated so far.[28]

Choi Sunu, the fourth director of NMK, was at the centre of this nationalist orientation. Indeed, Choi had searched for the independent value of Korean culture since he joined NMK in 1946. In his firm nationalist orientation, he was confident that the Japanese rule had demolished and distorted Korean culture. Ever since Choi, who was from Gaeseong, met Go Yu-seop, the first Korean art historian and director of the Gaeseong Municipal Museum, he was an admirer. After Go's death in 1944, Choi joined the museum in 1945. With the museum annexed to NMK in 1946, he became a member of the National Museum of Korea. Choi, even though he did not acquire an academic degree, contributed his short essays on ceramics to newspapers beginning in the early 1950s, and his earnest research and participation in the excavation of ceramic kilns in the 1960s made him an unrivalled specialist in that field (Ahn, 2000, pp. 291–304).

However, he was not satisfied to remain a specialist on Korean ceramics. He pursued a comprehensive understanding of Korean beauty and Korean culture. His ambition was influenced by Go Yu-seop, who wanted to build the edifice of Korean art history as the first Korean art historian. Go's ethnic nationalist orientation also influenced Choi. In an interview with a magazine, Choi recollected that Go had recommended that he study Korean art history, mentioning that:

> Korean youths under the Dark Age have various ways of contributing to the ethnic nation. The ancient art of Korea is an extraordinary

> existence and will be necessarily re-evaluated. It is very important to build the edifice of Korean art and make the ethnic nation recognise their pride properly.[29]

About 50 years later, Choi became the director of NMK, and he asserted, in the preface of a catalogue published in 1978, that the "Korean people have built an independent culture and foundation of history as a genuine ethnic nation, and have firmly preserved our beautiful land and language" (Choi, 1978, p. 1). His remark clearly shows his firm orientation toward ethnic nationalism as a basis of interpretation of cultural objects.

Westernisation brought on by fast industrialisation was being considered as another obstacle in discovering, interpreting and appreciating Korean material culture. Choi was a person of literary talent. His numerous contributions on various genres of Korean arts to newspapers and magazines were so eloquent that they played an important role in arousing the ethnic national sensitivity of the populace. In a sense, his thinking was well in accordance with the ethnic nationalist policy of the government. A narrative in 1973, by a high-ranking government official, reveals this accordance:

> The large scale of the investment of the government budget is not simply for administering the collection of NMK. Its real meaning is in giving Korean nationals pride as a civilised, ethnic nation by helping them appreciate our ancestors' great accomplishments and understand our history and tradition through the exhibition of cultural heritage, which contains the hearts of our ethnic nation in this magnificent building.[30]

The ultimate intention of this narrative, national unity, is explained clearly by a remark in 1974 by Yun Ju-yeong (born in 1928), the minister of the Ministry of Culture and Information. In the preface to a catalogue of Korean art works published by the Office of Cultural Properties, he emphasised that "to inherit traditional culture and art and to create new culture and art is for building a sound social ethos and cultivating cooperative national character by familiarising people's everyday life with art, the essence of national emotion." He added, "Here the introduced essences of 5,000 years of ethnic national culture would arouse a sense of duty in revitalising culture and art, and in displaying our proud ethnic national art all over the world" (Office of Cultural Properties, 1974, p. 1). Indeed, NMK made it one of its major missions of the year 1974 to display ethnic national culture abroad through the international exchange exhibition. Government authorities and NMK gained confidence from positive responses to the exhibition of *Two Thousand Years of Korean Art*. It led to another large-scale overseas special exhibition in Japan in 1976.

In search of ethnic national identity: Exhibitions and investigations of NMK in the 1970s

The mission of the year 1970 for NMK was to contribute "to the establishment of the ethnic national subjectivity by collecting, keeping, displaying and researching our cultural heritage."[31] This definition properly reflected the government's ethnic, nationalist drive, and it also suggested the direction and purpose of the detailed tasks of NMK. First of all, special exhibitions were intended for the search of national identity through each genre of art. In the 1970s, NMK organised a series of special exhibitions whose title began with the word "Korean," such as *Masterpieces of 500 Years of Korean Painting* (1972), *2000 Years of Korean Arts* (1973), *Korean Prehistoric Bronze Artefacts* (1973), *Korean Folk Art* (1975), *Korean Classical Embroidery* (1978), *Korean Portraits* (1979) and *Korean Calligraphy* (1980) (NMK, 2006, p. 143). This tendency from 1972 clearly showed that NMK was striving to forge the cultural identity of Korea, and that it was trying to make people recognise the material culture as concrete evidence of the reality of the ethnic nation (Figure 3.2). In this sense, the following remark in the preface of the catalogue of the exhibition entitled *Korean Portraits* is memorable: "We ask ourselves who we are in order to restore the righteous spirit of our ethnic nation and ethnic national culture" (NMK, 2006, p. 143).

Shedding new light on the material culture of the Joseon dynasty also was vital in order to overcome the colonial view of Korean history. NMK focused on authentic genres such as painting and porcelain. A series of special exhibitions related to such genres were held during the 1960s, and NMK actively pursued the discovery and introduction of detailed themes of those genres. NMK held a series of special exhibitions related to Korean paintings, including *Masterpieces of 500 Years of Korean Painting*, *Undisclosed Paintings in the Custody of the National Museum of Korea* (1977) and *Korean Portraits*, in order to demonstrate the cultural capacity of the Joseon dynasty. In addition, it is noteworthy that the catalogue of all of the special exhibitions began to be published after the catalogue of the *Masterpieces of 500 Years of Korean Painting* was first published in 1972 (Figure 3.2).

The academic investigations undertaken by NMK during the 1970s focused on relics of prehistoric ages such as the Neolithic, Bronze and Early Iron ages (NMK, 2006, pp. 170–82), while the Office of Cultural Properties concentrated on the relics of the Three Kingdoms period, especially on ancient royal relics such as tombs and palaces in Gyeongju. NMK pursued a long history of the ethnic nation from the prehistoric ages, while the Office of Cultural Properties searched for evidence of the golden ages from the royal relics of ancient kingdoms, especially in Gyeongju. From 1971 to 1975,

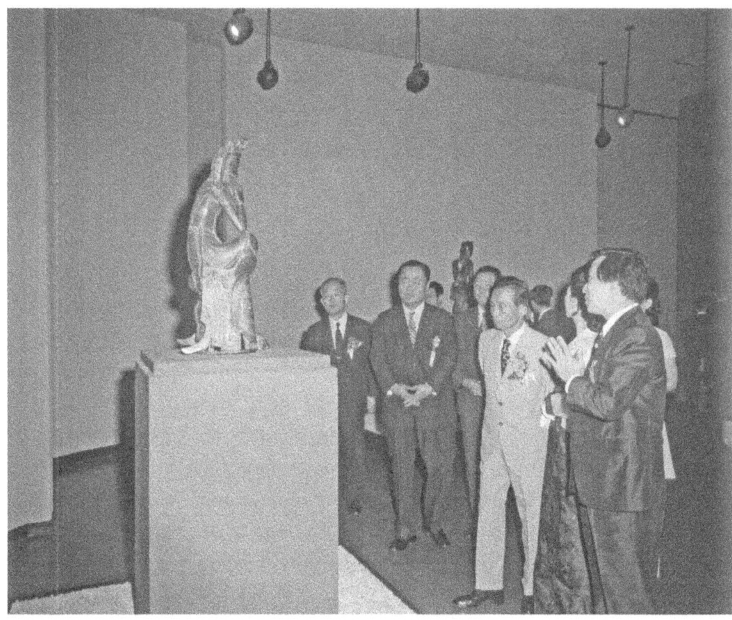

Figure 3.2 President Park Chung Hee at the reopening ceremony of the National Museum of Korea in Gyeongbokgung Palace in August 1972. With kind permission from the National Archives of Korea.

NMK's excavation of dwelling sites of the Neolithic Age at Amsa-dong in Seoul and Sinam-ri in Ulsan city greatly contributed to understanding the Neolithic Age. NMK's investigation of dwelling sites of the Bronze Age in Songguk-ri in Buyeo from 1975 to 1978 also played an important role in establishing cultural aspects of the age in Korea. Furthermore, a discovery of typical hand-axes at a Palaeolithic site at Jeongok-ri in Yeoncheon, north of Seoul, meant the complete establishment of images of the prehistoric age in the Korean peninsula (NMK, 2006, pp. 170–1).

These relics of the Three Kingdoms Period excavated by the Office of Cultural Properties yielded far more artefacts than expected. NMK contributed to drawing ethnic national pride from newly excavated artefacts by holding four special exhibitions: *Muryeong Wangneung* (royal tomb of the Baekje dynasty, 1971), *Renowned Treasures of the Silla Dynasty* (1974), *Silla Ssangbun* (the twin tombs of the Silla dynasty, 1975) and *Anapji* (royal pond of Silla dynasty, 1980) (NMK, 2006, p. 143). In the same context, from 1964 to 1984, NMK excavated kiln sites of Goryeo celadon for a systematic understanding of Goyreo celadon, which was considered one of the finest examples of cultural heritage at home and abroad. The investigation of a kiln site by NMK especially focused especially on sites of Goryeo celadon kiln during the 1970s.

Cultural diplomacy and display of national identity abroad

2000 Years of Korean Art in Japan

The special exhibition in 1973, *2000 Years of Korean Art*, was intended to inspire South Koreans with their cultural identity, reflecting the confidence of the government, NMK and South Korean academics in building a national identity through Korean material culture. This exhibition was also enough to draw the attention of the Japanese academic circle. Their interest in Korean culture resulted from the close relations between Japanese and Korean ancient culture. They realised that they should review Korean ancient culture in order to understand their own ancient culture, because the cultural influences from the Korean peninsula were made clearer by a series of new archaeological discoveries in both Japan and Korea from the early 1970s (Jang, 2015, pp. 168–71).

The loan exhibition from the South Korean government, however, was triggered by the diplomatic background. Since the normalisation of diplomatic relations between South Korea and Japan in 1965, the two countries developed a close relationship through their anti-communist position in the Far East, and Japanese economic aid was essential to the development of the South Korean economy (Kimiya, 2011, pp. 18–19). Two diplomatically sensitive incidents that took place between the two countries in 1973 and 1974, respectively, delayed its realisation, so that those incidents made both governments find more practical diplomatic uses of the exhibition (Jang, 2015, pp. 171–3).

On 8 August 1973, the former presidential candidate in the 1971 election, Kim Dae-jung (1924–2009, president of Republic of Korea from 1998 to 2003), was kidnapped in Tokyo, allegedly by the South Korean intelligence agency. He was staging an anti-Park regime movement in the US and Japan, and became disposable. However, he survived, thanks to the US government's pressure on the South Korean government (Kim, 2011, pp. 64–71). Both the South Korean and Japanese governments, in need of maintaining their close relations for each other's cooperation in economic terms, did not want this incident to become a diplomatic issue, but the Japanese press and civilian society criticised both governments, arguing that Japanese sovereignty was infringed by the South Korean government.

Another incident was the assassination of the South Korean first lady, Yuk Yeong-su (1925–1974), by a Korean resident in Japan on 15 August 1974.

This incident resulted in fierce antipathy towards the Japanese government because the assassin utilised a forged Japanese passport when entering South Korea, and used a gun which he had stolen from the Japanese police. The South Korean government even suggested severing diplomatic relations (Kimiya, 2011, p. 45). These two incidents blocked the normal supply of the development loan which the South Korean government was keen on getting from Japan for economic development.

The visit to Seoul of the minister for Japanese Foreign Affairs, Miyajawa Kiichi (1919–2007), on 23 July 1975 eliminated those long-standing obstacles, normalising the diplomatic relations between two countries (Balfe, 1987, p. 213). This diplomatic settlement eliminated the last barrier to the exhibition, and at the same time provided a strong stimulus to the promotion of this project. Indeed, events for establishing friendship between both countries were needed, one of which was the exhibition.

On 4 October 1975, the minister of Culture and Information submitted the bill for the overseas exhibition to the cabinet council of the South Korean government.[32] This bill gave two reasons why this exhibition, *5000 Years of Korean Art*, was needed. The first was the active request from Japan and the second was the need to promote the right understanding and recognition between both nations by displaying the superiority of Korean culture and its influence on Japanese culture. The cabinet council passed it on 7 October 1975. The three participating institutions consisted of the Kyoto National Museum, the Fukuoka Prefecture Culture Centre and the Tokyo National Museum. The Kyoto National Museum, whose director had been most active in hosting this exhibition since 1973, became the first venue of the exhibition. This exhibition would exhibit 343 artefacts in total, including 44 national treasures, and was the biggest in scale in the history of overseas exhibitions. These artefacts were collected from 15 institutions, as well as from 13 private collectors.[33]

The South Korean government wanted to utilise this overseas exhibition as much as it could. Its domestic propaganda on the exhibition was quite appealing and successful. The government's explanation that this exhibition would give ethnic national pride to the Korean residents in Japan also had its appeal. Choi Sunu was the right person to complete this mission. Now in his late 50s, he had spent his adolescence under Japanese colonial rule, and had grown to become an art historian with the most representative ethnic nationalist perspective. He conveyed the emotion he felt when he attended the opening ceremony at the Kyoto National Museum:

> I have not thought of this *5000 Years of Korean Art* only for the ostentation of our culture, or as a simple international event for friendship. I wanted to make the Japanese people realise that our ethnic nation has

> had a creative position and role in Asian art by explaining its cultural achievements, especially a stream of the formative arts which our ethnic nation has made during its long, 5000-year history from prehistory to the Joseon dynasty. This exhibition is essential because it represents the most basic and adequate effort to shake the long roots of Japanese prejudice against Koreans and the history between Korea and Japan.[34]

Although NMK defined the purpose of exhibition in Japan as "contributing to friendship between both nations,"[35] it is clear that Choi Sunu's emphasis on the superiority of Korean culture was directly related to a sense of rivalry with Japanese culture and his strong will to recover ethnic national pride by displaying Korean national identity through its material culture. As shown in the permanent exhibition in 1972 and the 1973 special exhibition *2000 Years of Korean Art*, NMK and South Korean academics managed to construct a concrete shape of the ethnic national culture, thanks to a series of ethnic nationalist government policies and their own efforts. This circumstance was quite different from when the first overseas exhibition had taken place in the US (Jang, 2016, pp. 464–6; Lin, 2016, pp. 388–9).

This overseas exhibition, especially in Japan, which had colonised Korea, offered a special and strong chance for the ethnic nationalist interpretation of cultural objects to reach its peak. The catalogue of this exhibition describes this situation very well. Seven South Korean academics contributed to this catalogue, with each contributor writing on an overview of Korean history and each writing introductions to the six art genres, unlike the catalogue of the first overseas Korean exhibition in the US in 1957, to which no Korean scholar contributed. This change meant that South Korean scholars had assimilated the academic outcomes of their material culture since the liberation, and had asserted their own voices on their own "ethnic national" culture.

This overseas exhibition, which opened on 23 February 1976 at the Kyoto National Museum, toured two more cities, Fukuoka and Tokyo, until 25 July 1976, attracting 573,201 people in total. In the complementary comment in the exhibition catalogue, Miki Takeo (1907–1988), the prime minister of the Japanese government, said:

> It is needless to say that Korea is the nearest neighbouring country to Japan, and that Korea has kept the closest connection with Japan from the ancient era. This geographical and historical connection also helped us to learn many things in the cultural field, indeed. … We are quite pleased to expect that these precious Korean historical cultural properties to be first introduced in Japan will promote our understanding of ethnic national culture.[36]

His comment is representative of the basic tone of the Japanese press towards the exhibition (Jang, 2015, pp. 179–83).

The South Korean press was satisfied with the Japanese favourable responses and conveyed them to the South Korean public. In an article entitled "Prejudice on Korean Culture Was Washed Away," *The Chosunilbo* commented that this exhibition gave to the Japanese archaeologists and historians a chance to correct and show regret for their wrong views which they had regarding the history of Korea.[37] After the touring exhibition in Japan had finished and come back to Korea, NMK held the homecoming exhibition, displayed the "national" cultural artefacts that the Japanese people had "admired," and promoted the internalisation of them by the Korean public.

5000 Years of Korean Art in the US

The success of this Korean art exhibition in Japan led to the touring exhibition in the US from May 1979 to September 1981. In the late 1970s, the US was the most suitable country for conducting cultural diplomacy with the South Korean government. As in the Japanese case, diplomatic tensions between the two countries made both establish cultural events to alleviate those tensions, while delaying the discussion and influencing the process of the exhibition (Jang, 2015, pp. 183–5). The tensions between South Korea and the US were more practical and critical than the ones between South Korea and Japan. On 24 October 1976, *The Washington Post* reported that a South Korean lobbyist, Park Dong-sun, and the South Korean Intelligence Agency, under the direction of President Park, offered bribes worth from US$500,000 to $1 million to members of the US Congress (Moon, 1994, p. 247). Called "Koreagate," this incident disrupted the relationship between both countries for two years, even though the South Korean government absolutely denied any wrongdoing.

Behind this lobbying or corruption lay the diplomatic needs of the South Korean government, which wanted to secure as much national security from the US as possible, in response to Nixon's troop withdrawal policy (Cumings, 2005, pp. 459–61). With the US political circles beginning to consider the issue as essential in keeping the US's allies safe, the issue of human rights in South Korea became another obstacle in getting aid from the US. Although the US government ultimately admitted in 1981 that it should put the security of allied nations before human rights issues, the Carter government (1977–1981) and the US Congress urged considering the issues as a prerequisite of US aid. President Jimmy Carter's policy of withdrawing the US ground forces from South Korea was also a threat to the South Korean government, although it did not happen.

Koreagate resulted in conflicts between the South Korean government and the US Congress, over the issue of attendance at the hearings of the parliament of lobbyist Park Dong-seon and Kim Dong-jo, the then South Korean diplomat to Washington allegedly implicated in Koreagate. The South Korean government was reluctant to send them to the hearing and, to this end, refused to send Kim, who had diplomatic immunity. By rejecting a series of military and economic aid demands from South Korea, the US Congress put pressure on the South Korean government. However, the government withstood the pressure. On 19 August 1978, Koreagate was settled according to an agreement between both sides that Kim Dong-jo would submit a written answer to the hearing (Moon, 1994, pp. 247–300).

In April 1977, Rene-Yvon Lefebre d'Argence, the director of the Asian Art Museum of San Francisco, proposed an arrangement for the US touring exhibition.[38] It meant that this touring exhibition project resumed amid the vortex of diplomatic tensions between South Korea and the US. It seems that the South Korean government approached this issue just as it had the precedent with Japan in 1976. In December 1978, after the settlement of Koreagate, Choi Sunu and d'Argence finally signed the exhibition agreement.[39]

Not only national security but also exports to the US were essential to South Korea, which pushed forward with an export-centred economic development strategy. The US was the biggest market for South Korea (Eckert, 1990b, pp. 395–9). In 1970, 48.2 per cent of South Korea's exports were to the US. In 1975, exports to the US increased by 382 percent over 1970. In 1980, South Korea exported merchandise worth US$46 billion to the US (Moon, 1994, p. 207). The Ministry of Foreign Affairs of South Korea reported on measures linking *5000 Years of Korean Art* with an increase in exports to the US at the third Export Promotion Conference in April 1979.[40] In fact, 15 South Korean companies sponsored and supported the touring exhibition financially. These South Korean sponsors included major companies such as the Samsung Group and the Hyundai Business Group.[41]

The exhibition *5000 Years of Korean Art*, which toured eight cities in the US from May 1979 to September 1981, attracted 2,262,138 visitors (Figure 3.3).[42] The total audience increased 13.5 times in comparison with the first overseas exhibition in 1957, which attracted only 167,731 visitors. This exhibition was the largest in the number of exhibits in the history of the South Korean government's overseas exhibitions. The government sent 354 items, including 46 national treasures, 31 percent of which were from 17 private collectors.[43] The selection of artefacts was very discreet, and demand for participants was persistent. This atmosphere showed how the selection committee was eager to select the best masterpieces. It meant that the members of the committee were highly conscious of American scholars' response, and intended to display outcomes which the Korean academic circle had accumulated since the liberation (Jang, 2015, pp. 189–94).

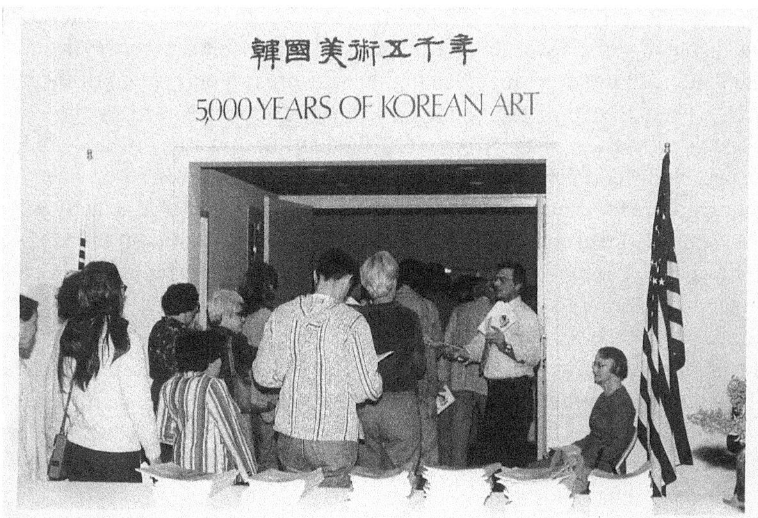

Figure 3.3 5000 Years of Korean Art in San Francisco in 1979. Copyright unknown.

The catalogue of this exhibition explains how actively South Korean academics were engaged in this exhibition. As the acknowledgements in this catalogue showed, this well-organised catalogue "required the unselfish participation of an unusually large number of Korean, American and Canadian scholars."[44] These South Korean scholars consisted of two groups: the members of the selection committee, who began their research with self-study after the liberation; and young scholars who earned doctoral degrees in art history from American universities. The former group included Kim Won-yong, Choi Sunu, Hwang Su-yeong, Jin Hong-seop and Yun Mu-byeong. The latter group included Ahn Hwi-jun (PhD, Princeton University), Kim Lena (PhD, Harvard University), Yi Song-mi (doctoral candidate, Princeton University) and Kim Kumja (doctoral candidate, Stanford University). The South Korean academic circle's confidence in their academic accumulation was supported by the young scholars who had absorbed the academic methodology of American scholarship. As seen in the exhibition catalogue, this exhibition deepened the chronological approach on Korean material culture which had already been attempted in the exhibition in Japan, with each art genre organised by dynasty (Lin, 2016, pp. 391–2).

The South Korean press also looked for favourable comments on the exhibition and persistently introduced them to the South Korean public.[45]

When the exhibition began in San Francisco, the *Kyunghyang Shinmun* reported that this event would renew the view on South Korea of Americans by displaying the essence of Korean traditional culture, conveying that the American press commended highly on Korean's enjoyment of diverse arts.[46] This attitude of the South Korean press is exemplified by the titles of news articles, such as "Wonderful! Wonderful! Towards brilliant golden crowns and Buddhist statues"[47] and "Echo of extolment wherever the exhibition goes."[48] Indeed, this kind of responses from the US was exactly what the South Korean government wanted. When the exhibition ended, Lee Gwang-pyo, the minister of Culture and Information, issued the following statement in order to celebrate its success:

> I report to our nation that the exhibition *5000 Years of Korean Art* was widely welcomed by the US government and the public and produced satisfactory results. This exhibition made Americans recognise that Koreans have a distinctive and creative art, different from Chinese or Japanese art. Furthermore, in the international symposiums held during the tour, American intellectuals and art specialists got to find a new world of beauty which they had not been aware of. In addition, this exhibition gave a chance for major American museums to establish or enlarge permanent galleries for Korean art. Now scholars who are willing to research Korean culture are increasing.[49]

This statement also explains which message the government wanted to convey to South Koreans. The government was reaffirming that South Korea was recognised by the US as an ethnic nation-state with a clear cultural identity. On returning from the US, the national treasures were again displayed in a homecoming exhibition at NMK from 9 November to 6 December 1981.[50] It meant that a cultural identity clearly different from neighbouring nations was intended to be internalised as values which should be pursued by South Koreans.

This second overseas exhibition, *5000 Years of Korean Art*, was organised in a period of strong ethnic nationalist policies under President Park's regime. Ethnic nationalism became a systematic ideology, and all of the cultural artefacts were systematically being put in order under the name of ethnic nation. NMK and South Korean scholars were keen on securing a positive evaluation from American academics and public on the exhibition and the academic capital that they had accumulated. As director Choi Sunu said, the second overseas exhibition was an effort to achieve recognition of the independent perspectives and researches of Korean academics, and to display the cultural identity of Korea.[51]

Notes

1 Cho argues that Rhee sought to expand the basis of consent to his rule only through the anti-communism of the 1950s.

2 Lee claims that Rhee Syngman, as a veteran of the independence movement and founder of the republic of Korea, had charisma that the South Korean people voluntarily acknowledged.

3 Cho argues that Park utilised both anti-communism and ethnic nationalism as representative ideological justifications for his dictatorship. However, Cho describes Park's ethnic nationalism as a pseudo-ethnic nationalism for the reason that his ethnic nationalism was in essence confronting the ethnic nation.

4 *The Kyunghyang Shinmun*, 7 July 1961.

5 "Bak uijang sinnyeonsa [Acting President Park's New Year's Address]," *The Dong-A Ilbo*, 1 January 1962.

6 Park Chung Hee, "Chuiimsa [Inaugural Address]," 17 December 1963. Available at: http://pa.go.kr/research/contents/speech/index.jsp. Accessed 16 January 2019.

7 "Minjokmunhwa ui yusan eul sojunghi bojonhaja [Let Us Cherish Heritage of the Ethnic National Culture]," *The Kyunghyang Shinmun* (2 November 1961); "Munhwajae bohobeop jejeong ui sigeupseong [Urgency of Enactment of Cultural Objects Preservation Act]," *The Dong-A Ilbo* (29 December 1961).

8 Park said, "We should not just preserve cultural objects as relics covered with lichens, but, through this festival, gather all the efforts with which we could heighten the standards of ethnic national restoration for reforming our present and future." See *The Kyunghyang Shinmun*, 21 April 1962.

9 NMK, "Eopmu hyeonhwang [Status Report]," July 1962, pp. 47–52. In comparison, this systemised definition of the tasks of NMK was not seen in status reports before 1962.

10 NMK, "Hyeonhwang bogo [Status Report]," October 1963, pp. 14–16.

11 A leaflet published in 1969 explained that the collection of NMK consisted of both ethnic national cultural objects and foreign cultural objects. See NMK, "Gungnip bangmulgwan [National Museum of Korea]," 1969.

12 Increases in budget and manpower in 1969 resulted from the annexation of the Deoksugung Museum of Art by NMK.

13 Park Chung Hee, "Jonghap bangmulgwan gigongsik chisa [Congratulatory Speech at the Ground-breaking Ceremony for the General Museum]," 22 November 1966. Available at: http://pa.go.kr/research/contents/speech/index.jsp. Accessed 16 January 2019. In 1965 the government planned to construct a series of national cultural institutions such as an art museum and theatre. It called these plans the General Cultural Centre project. The new NMK building was also constructed as one part of this project.

14 Ibid.

15 Choi remarked that Park's view reflected his political ambition and the colonial view of Korean history.

16 NMK, *Cheongdong yumul dorok* [Selected Bronze Objects of the Early Metal Period in Korea 1945-1968], Seoul, 1968. Prior to this publication, NMK had published a catalogue titled *Jinyeolpum dogam* [Selected Museum Exhibits 1945–1965] in 1965. These publications were intended to organise NMK's academic achievements since the liberation.

17 NMK, "1970 nyeondo eopmubogo [Status Report of the Year 1970]," p. 9.

18 Ahn Hwi-jun, a renowned Korean art historian, argued that the field of Korean paintings was much damaged by the colonial view of Korean history. He added that this was why many foreign scholars kept some prejudices about Korean paintings. See Ahn Hwi-jun, *Hanguk hoehwasa* [A History of Korean Paintings], Seoul: Iljisa, 1980, pp. 1–4.

19 Park Chung Hee, "Chwiimsa [Inaugural Address]," 1 July 1971. Available at: http://pa.go.kr/research/contents/speech/index.jsp. Accessed 16 January 2019.

20 "Munye jungheung seoneonmun [Declaration for Revitalising Culture and Art]," *The Dong-A Ilbo*, 20 October 1973.

21 *The Kyunghyang Shinmun*, 23 November 1972.

22 The theme of the ten galleries were as follows: Prehistory period; Goguryeo and Packche Dynasties (Three Kingdoms period); Silla dynasty (Three Kingdoms period); The Unified Silla dynasty; Ceramics of the Goryeo dynasty; Ceramics of the Yi (Joseon) dynasty; Painting and Calligraphy; Buddhist sculpture; Buddhist Metal Arts; and Metal Craft. See NMK, 1972, p. 154.

23 Anon., "Jinyeolsil haeseol [Introduction to the galleries]," *Bangmulgwan shinmun* (The Museum News) vol.24, NMK, November 1972, p. 3.

24 *Bangmulgwan shinmun*, vol.33, November 1973, pp. 1–2; NMK, "Eopmu hyeonhwang [Status Report]," January 1974, p. 9; This exhibition was based on the archaeological accumulation of the 1960s, such as *Cheongdong yumul dorok* [Selected Bronze Objects of the Early Metal Period in Korea 1945–1968] published in 1968.

25 Sekino first investigated a tomb of Nangnang in Pyongyang in 1909, although he thought it belonged to the Goguryeo Kingdom. During colonial period, the Japanese scholars concluded that they found in the Pyongyang area the Chinese culture transmitted directly from China proper (Oh, 2006, pp. 16–17).

26 This recognition also followed the former director Kim Chewon's thinking. After retirement, Kim published a book entitled *Arts of Korea*. In its introduction, he wrote that "the Yi (dynasty's) system provided but little allowance for free thinking, creative artistry." See Kim Chewon and Lee Kim Lena, *Arts of Korea*, Tokyo: Kodansha International Ltd., 1974, p. 19.

27 NMK, "Eopmu hyeonhwang [Status Report]," January 1974, p. 9.

28 *Bangmulgwan shinmun*, vol.45, January 1975, p. 1.

29 Choi Sunu, "Jeontong iran jagijasin [Tradition is One's Own Self]," *Saemteo*, November 1981.

30 *Bangmulgwan shinmun*, vol.25, January 1973, p. 4.

31 NMK, "Eopmu bogo [Status Report]," January 1970, p. 9.

32 Ministry of Culture and Information, "Munhwajae haeoe jeonsi leul wihan banchul [Export of the Cultural Properties for the Overseas Exhibition]" (Bill no.1015), 4 October 1975. See also Jang, 2015, pp. 173–5.

33 Anon., "Hanguk misul ocheonnyeon [5000 Years of Korean Art]," *Bangmulgwan sinmun*, vol.55, January 1976, p. 2.

34 Sunu Choi, "Hanguk misul ocheonnyeon jeon eul yeoleo noko [After Opening the *5000 Years of Korean Art*]," *Bangmulgwan shinmun*, vol.57, 1 April 1976, p. 1.

35 Anon., "Ilboneseo yeollineun hanguk misul ocheonnyeon jeon [5000 Years of Korean Art which Will Be Exhibited in Japan], vol.53, 1 November 1975, p. 1.

36 Miki Takeo, "Shukuji [Congratulatory Message]," in Tokyo National Museum et al., *Kankoku bijutsu gosennen* [5000 Years of Korean Art].

37 *The Chosunilbo*, 20 April 1976.

38 "News Release," 19 February 1979, The Asian Art Museum of San Francisco.

39 The cabinet council of the South Korean Government passed the bill for the overseas exhibition in the US on 2 March 1979.

40 Anon., "Hanguk misul ocheonnyeon jeon miguk jeon e bucheoseo [Towards *5000 Years of Korean Art in the US*]," *The Chosunilbo*, 1 May 1979.

41 Korean Overseas Information Service, *Collection of the Press Articles Related to 5000 Years of Korean Art in San Francisco*, 1979, p. 177.

42 This overseas exhibition, which opened on 1 May 1979 at the Asian Art Museum of San Francisco, toured seven more cities, Seattle (Seattle Art Museum), Chicago (The Art Institute of Chicago), Cleveland (Cleveland Museum of Art), Boston (Museum of Fine Arts), New York (The Metropolitan Museum of Art), Kansas City (William Rockhill Nelson Gallery) and Washington, DC (National Museum of Natural History), until 15 September 1981. See Jang, 2015, p. 195.

43 Asian Art Museum of San Francisco, *5000 Years of Korean Art*, San Francisco, 1979.

44 Ibid., p. 10.

45 For example, *The Kyunghyang Shinmun* reported on an article in the *Los Angeles Times* of 13 May 1979 (*The Kyunghyang Shinmun*, 26 May 1979).

46 *The Kyunghyang Shinmun*, 9 May 1979.

47 Anon., "nunbusin geumgwan bulsang e wondeopul tto wondeopul [Wonderful! Wonderful! Towards Brilliant Golden Crowns and Buddhist Statues]," *The Kyunghyang Shinmun*, 9 May 1979.

48 *The Seoul Shinmun*, 22 August 1980.

49 Ministry of Culture and Information, "Janggwan damhwa [A Statement by the Minister]," October 1981.

50 *Bangmulgwan shinmun*, vol.124, December 1981.

51 Choi Sunu, "Migugin ui hanguk siya lul neolpyeotta [Americans' Widened Perspective on Korea]," *The HanKook Ilbo*, 2 October 1981. From February 1984 to January 1985, *5000 Years of Korean Art* toured three Western European cities, London, Hamburg and Cologne. See Horlyck & Priewe, 2018, pp. 97–100.

4 National narrative and South Korean society

The South Korean government tried to construct the increasingly essentialised and controlled communication of the national narrative directed towards South Korean society, especially from the 1970s. In this drive, NMK played an important role in this process. In 1980, South Korea had a new authoritarian government, whose leader, Chun Doo-hwan, had grasped power through a military coup in December 1979. Under this regime, NMK continued to put forth a pro-nationalist policy through its exhibitions and education programmes. It was in this context that NMK was reinvented in 1986, in the former Government-General's building, where it displayed its 40-year-long accomplishments in constructing Korean cultural identity using material culture. The demolition of this building and temporary relocation of NMK in 1996, and the reopening of NMK in 2005 in the Yongsan area, in the centre of the capital, Seoul, showed how ethnic national sensitivity could have a tremendous influence on South Korean society, especially when the issues were related to Japanese colonial rule.

Museum education in the 1970s

Only a few documents on NMK museum education have survived from the 1960s, which may show that museum education hardly drew any fully-fledged attention from either the museum or the government, despite the government's nationalist intention to utilise the museum. The second director, Kim Won-yong (in office from 1970 to 1971), took a meaningful step forwards and published the first issue of a monthly newsletter, *Bangmulgwannyuus* [The Museum News], in October 1970, to introduce museum activities geared towards the public and academics. The installation of a suggestion box in the museum at the time of the appointment of director Kim Won-yong was also a symbolic gesture, showing the museum's efforts to communicate with visitors.[1]

Along with these actions, the museum staff began to raise questions about descriptive labels, which showed that they were pondering the effective methods of conveying their discourse on ethnic culture.[2] In his inauguration address in October 1971, the third director, Hwang Su-yeong (in office from 1971 to 1974), expressed his intention to attract the participation of the public in activities at the museum, promising to diminish the distance between the museum and everyday citizens. His remarks anticipated the expansion of the education programme. The following comment by a curatorial staff member of NMK in 1972 shows that the curators became aware of the need to expand the education programme:

> I feel that a museum visit should be more concrete and richer in content because it has a meaning as on-the-spot learning rather than as a touristic curiosity. It is needless to say that museums should have an adequate system and a scale of a social education institution. Holding seminars for professionals, providing academic resources and giving gallery talks to the public can be proposed, but lectures and guidance for children should be provided more rapidly than anything else.[3]

The drastic increase in manpower and budget in 1972 made these ideas realised. As Hwang said, "It is not until 20 years ago that the development of and change [in NMK] began, and that the expansion of national strength became conducive to the expansion of the roles of NMK."[4] In June 1973, museum special lectures for teachers began with a new scheme,[5] and the Cultural Objects Drawing Contest for Children made a start in October 1974.[6] Both projects were set up to instil a sense of the superiority of Korean ethnic national culture and infuse national pride. In this context, education programmes began to be designed also for those other than students. For example, lectures were prepared for spouses of diplomats dispatched to overseas embassies, and to foreign nationals residing in the Seoul area, to help them understand Korean material culture.[7] The library for staff members in NMK was also opened for audiences on June 1973.[8]

As participation by the public in the museum activities became an important issue, a civilian organisation, Friends of the National Museum of Korea, was established on 9 September 1974. This organisation, in which museum enthusiasts and benefactors participated, aimed to be "an aid, tangible or intangible, to NMK, by promoting the participation of civilians in museum activities, and by assisting with such fields that a governmental institution such as NMK cannot intervene directly."[9] The establishment of this organisation showed that the opinion makers in the field of culture began to take the lead in supporting the discourse on ethnic national culture on the basis of pride in their material culture, by attracting voluntary participation of the public.

Experiencing a drastic increase in audiences with the success of the opening of permanent galleries in Seoul in 1972 and the exhibition *2000*

Years of Korean Art in 1973, as shown in Table 4.1, Choi Sunu concluded that this success resulted from "the increase in interest of the public in our ancestors' cultural heritage." He added,

> NMK reached a standard of famous world class museums, thanks to the rapid increase in audiences, and this success is very meaningful in that the nation's attention was directed to NMK in accordance with the development of the museum and the increase of our national strength.[10]

Indeed, the increase in audiences in this period came from the heightened interest in traditional culture as a consequence of the influence of the diffusion of the discourse of ethnic national culture and the success of economic development. It is no less important that the government encouraged students to visit the museum. Another factor was the increase in the number of tourists in local cities such as Gyeongju, Buyeo and Gongju, all of which had local branch museums. This promotion of tourism also resulted from the government's strong drive in 1974 to develop these ancient historic cities as centres of tourism. In terms of these changes, Choi Sunu said:

> researchers or applicants for art history or archaeology courses unprecedentedly increased. Especially, the number of people who have knowledge of traditional art, or who claim to have it, has increased a lot. This is why we cannot help being criticised.[11]

Table 4.1 Visitors to NMK, 1961 to 1979

Year	*Seoul*	*Gyeongju*	*Buyeo*	*Gongju*	*Gwangju*	*Folk Museum (Seoul)*	*Total*
1961	55,231	116,407	20,313	1,570			193,521
1962	64,797	101,224	23,421	2,250			191,692
1967	103,558	211,781	40,219	4,273			359,831
1968	89,659	211,677	31,717	4,882			337,935
1969	79,969	209,789	42,689	4,969			337,416
1970	98,205	285,213	77,797	12,028			473,243
1971	186,349	402,239	138,360	29,479			756,427
1972	339,423	429,271	147,284	3,930			919,908
1973	619,187	611,172	199,515	36,220			1,466,094
1974	346,668	546,695	197,102	65,075		98,883	1,254,323
1975	387,442	528,800	218,043	67,936		101,662	1,303,883
1976	571,330	957,569	230,214	69,133		240,471	2,068,717
1977	537,707	993,502	259,840	86,461		203,769	2,081,279
1978	552,152	1,086,807	283,844	82,308	29,200	231,384	2,265,695
1979 (Jan to Aug)	412,490	793,427	191,766	65,433	202,983	175,157	1,841,256

Source: Ministry of Culture and Information, 1979, p. 326.

His remarks show that the 1970s met the creation of a layer of both specialists and appreciators. Furthermore, the private collecting of antiquities began to draw the upper classes' attention from this period.

However, criticisms from both inside and outside the museum also followed: the effectiveness of the message and its contents could not reach Koreans' expectations despite the expansion of education programmes. In the mid-1970s, NMK curatorial staff members pointed out several problems in telling audiences their stories, saying:

> it is clear that we have not yet devoted enough strength to the education activities. … We should appeal to the public's interests through the publication of guides without jargon, the diversification of the exhibitions' contents and the utilisation of the audio and visual materials.[12]

By contrast, these interests reflected the hope of South Koreans to overcome their dark and negative perspectives on their material culture which had resulted from the experiences of colonial rule and the rapid industrialisation in the 1970s. The following remark by Gang Seok-hui, a Korean composer who had studied in Germany, shows that even intellectuals were not exempt from this negative consciousness:

> It is often said that the beauty of Korea is characterised as simplicity. I have recognised this definition positively, but I often feel that such a definition shows a sort of inferiority complex. Sometimes, I hear that even academics agree to that definition as well as general civilians. Most Koreans feel our culture is trivial in comparison with the European culture we encounter when travelling in Europe.[13]

To wipe out this negative consciousness was one of the most important missions of NMK. The following comment on the missions of NMK by director Choi Sunu shows how his museum was engaged in changing the negative consciousness into a positive one:

> For the last 30 years we have newly acquired numerous cultural heritage artefacts and secured vivid materials of ancient history by excavating ancient relics, including prehistoric ones. On the basis of these resources, we should reconstruct ancient history, which has been distorted, and find the Korean traditional beauty. And we need to do our best in order to make our Korean nationals understand our traditional culture, which has been isolated so far.[14]

Choi thought that NMK's mission should be to reconstruct the history of Korea and discover the traditional beauty of Korea by correcting its history and traditional culture, distorted by Japanese colonialists. He also emphasised the importance of teaching this traditional culture to the public. His definition of the mission was accurately in accordance with the policies of the government. A high-ranking government official also mentioned that "large-scale investment of the government budget in the national museum was for giving Korean nationals pride as a civilised ethnic nation."[15]

Another government official in the field of cultural administration pointed out the fundamental purpose of the cultural policies under Park's regime by stating that "culture has a meaning of voluntary social unity. It contributes to national unity as the energy of the development of the country."[16] Thus, how to convey the museum's narrative effectively to the public was considered one of the most important tasks of NMK after the reopening in 1972.

Chun Doo-hwan's regime and the "promotion of culture"

On 26 October 1979, Park Chung Hee was assassinated by his right-hand man, Kim Jae-gyu, the head of the South Korean Central Intelligence Agency (Eckert, 1990a, p. 365). Park's death gave South Koreans some hope and expectation of more political freedom. However, Major General Chun Doo-hwan and his new junta of army officers grasped power through a military coup in December 1979 and the military suppression of a demonstration for democracy in a major local city, Gwangju, in May 1980. As Eckert (1990a, pp. 376–7) says, Chun's coup and transition to civilian rule in 1979–1981 followed a pattern established earlier by Park Chung Hee in 1961–1963. One of them was to continue to emphasise ethnic national culture, faithfully following Park's ethnic nationalist policies in the cultural sector.

Although Chun's regime (1980–1988), the core force of which had been the elite guard for Park Chung Hee, was actually the continuation of Park's regime (Kim, 1999, pp. 232–4), it tried to show its differences from that of Park's regime by taking some political measures, such as an amendment of the constitution in October 1980. One of the important revisions was the single-term system for the presidency. As Eckert (1990a, pp. 376–7) points out, a number of minor but highly visible social changes, which included the abolition of curfew and the relaxation of the dress code for students, conveyed the impression of greater liberalisation.

The new constitution added a clause that the government should make an effort to ensure the inheritance and development of traditional culture and the promotion of ethnic national culture. It was clear that this clause was strongly influenced by the cultural policy of Park's government. This new government, however, tried to differentiate itself from Park's government by adding the issue to the constitution.[17] This action meant that the new government, which lacked political legitimacy, put forward the value of ethnic culture as a symbol of national integration. Moreover, it presented "educational renovation and promotion of culture" as one of its four catch phrases, the other three of which were "nativisation of democracy," "construction of a welfare society" and "realisation of a just society." Chun's regime intended to utilise this rhetoric to cope with the demand from South Korean society for more political freedom and greater equality. Chun actually offered neither to any substantial degree. Rather, his regime needed "the security forces, such as tens of thousands of young conscripts who were trained as riot troops," as Eckert (1990a, p. 378) points out.

It could be understood against this background that more visible cultural projects were needed. On 23 June 1981, the government announced its cultural policy, which consisted of five major policy stances: the establishment of cultural subjectivity; the distribution of cultural benefit for social welfare; the enhancement of creative cultural capability; the strengthening of the support system for development of culture; and the enhancement of the cultural role of social education.[18] The agenda of the establishment of subjectivity was inherited from Park's policy. In detail, the government planned some museum projects for enlarging "national consciousness towards the ethnic national culture." These projects included the establishment of the local branch museums of NMK in Jinju and Cheongju, as well as the construction of a new building for the National Museum of Contemporary Art in a southern area of Seoul. Those local museums were also intended for a distribution of cultural benefit. This cultural policy faithfully followed Park's ethnic national policy in demanding national unity through emphasis on ethnic national culture. It was also clear that Chun was reluctant to allow South Koreans more political freedom, because it could threaten his regime. However, his government moved forward, at least in rhetoric, in foregrounding concepts of welfare, distribution and social education.

However, the attraction of two major international sports tournaments in September and November 1981 – the Asian Games in 1986 and the Olympic Games in 1988 in Seoul – also provided the government with a strong motivation to expand the cultural infrastructure of South Korea. One of the major projects was the relocation of NMK to the former Government-General building, which had been utilised as the capitol building of the South Korean government since liberation. On 16 March 1982, Lee Jin-hui (born in 1932), the minister of Culture and Information, issued the following statement on the relocation of NMK:

> Keeping in mind bitter memories related to this building, the government is considering a plan to expand and develop NMK by adding another function of displaying the subjectivity of the ethnic nation,

> including the history of the striving for independence, to its existing function. Accordingly, NMK in the future, should collect, arrange and display processes of our ethnic nation's formation and development, especially its creative historical development and process of overcoming national crisis and struggle for independence. Secondly, NMK should display the creativity and subjectivity of our culture, and our ethnic nation's authenticity, on the basis of comparison with the Western and Eastern cultures, especially following the new recognition of the surrounding cultures in terms of our traditional culture. Thirdly, NMK should expand its function in order to be a place for social education, for giving correct recognition of our traditional culture to South Korean nationals, as well as to foreigners who would visit our country.[19]

He added that this museum would make South Korean nationals eager to create a new history and heighten their ethnic national pride and confidence. He also articulated the government's expectation that there would be a new recognition of "cultural [civilised] Korea" from foreigners who would visit South Korea for the 1986 Asian Games and the 1988 Olympic Games. And it was in the same context that another government official, interviewed by *The Dong-AIlbo*, mentioned that those international sports events made the government strive to expand the cultural infrastructure.[20]

The relocation and renovation of NMK was also explained in a way that the project was for eliminating remnants of Japanese colonial rule. This explanation reflected a criticism that the former building of the Government General, which symbolised the colonial rule, should not be used for the government of the independent country. The South Korean government actively utilised this cause for explaining the relocation of NMK into the building. A newspaper reported that this project was for cleaning up the remnants of the 36-year-long Japanese colonial rule and instilling a sense of the sovereignty of the ethnic nation.[21] It added that this action stemmed from President Chun's deep consideration for making the stronghold of colonial rule into a space of education in which to arouse ethnic national pride and subjectivity. This decision was not criticised at the time, as the authoritarian regime controlled South Korean society. It was glamorised as a mature approach by which to overcome the memory of colonial rule. However, this issue would prove to be controversial within at most 10 years, as shown in the demolition of the building in 1996 which was being used as the national museum.

South Korean society and museum education

Although South Korean society was under the Chun regime's authoritarian control in the first half of the 1980s, this society was changing, demanding more political freedom and economic equality. However, the regime could not avoid accepting those changes, for example, extending democracy and welfare towards South Korean nationals. However, those benefits were to be given from the government rather than gained by deserving nationals. Here was the ultimate gap between the regime and the people. Eckert (1990b, p. 388) described South Korea in the 1980s as: "a 1980s economic powerhouse – a factory to the world for everything from clothes, shoes, and electronic goods to steel, ships, and now even automobiles and semiconductors." A per capita GNP of $87 in 1962 increased drastically to $1,546 in 1979. It was against this background that a reporter at *The Kyunghyang Shinmun*, referring to the plan for the construction of a new building for the National Museum of Contemporary Art, wrote, "the time has come to decorate with culture and art us who have been eager to seek bread and meat, and have busied ourselves filling our stomachs with them."[22]

In 1981, 1,800 applicants rushed to NMK for a one-year-long Museum Special Lectures programme, as reported in *The Hangukkyongje Shinmun* [The Korea Economic Daily]. This even caused the museum to increase the capacity of the course from 300 to 500 people.[23] The interest of the press continued in this interesting social phenomenon. *The Dong-A Ilbo* reported that about 80 per cent of the attendees were housewives, and presented the course as one of the diverse examples of making good use of leisure.[24] Mentioning that the course had opened and been met with tremendous popularity, *The Kyunghyang Shinmun* also reported that 99 attendees were awarded for perfect attendance at the completion ceremony of the course, and that this fact reflected the high interest in and zeal for traditional culture.[25]

This Museum Special Lectures programme, organised by NMK in 1977, was the beginning of an in-depth education of the public in Korean culture. The curriculum of this one-year-long programme included 41 lectures in the fields of archaeology, anthropology, art history, museum studies and so forth. This programme enjoyed popularity from the start. Five hundred two people applied for this course; NMK had to increase its admittance from 40 to 220 people.[26] From 1977 on, many applicants had to wait to be admitted to the course. NMK adopted admission screening procedures similar to those used by universities, and this course was subtitled "Museum College" from the second year.

This trend shows that the public's interest in their material culture was clearly aroused around this period. It seems that this change resulted from several factors. First of all, Korea's economic stability, although not enjoyed by all South Koreans, encouraged them to find some meaningful ways of utilising their leisure time. Secondly, the middle classes began to worry about the side effects of rapid economic development, such as materialism and the blind pursuit of a Western-centric perspective. Indeed, they felt that they were losing something of their own for the sake of economic wealth. An editorial writer of *The Seoul Shinmun* described this West-oriented attitude as hunger for culture, especially for Western culture.[27] A contribution to *Bangmulgwan shinmun* [The Museum News] from a government official who worked for the Ministry of Culture and Information summarised what the South Korean public thought the problem was in terms of foreign cultures:

> We have lived without knowing about ourselves and have despised our culture by ourselves. We have created a great culture in history. However, recent ordeals and the convulsion of the political situation which our ethnic nation has faced, has made us accept foreign cultures without any criticism, and take pride in talking about foreign cultures, separating ourselves from our traditional culture.[28]

This kind of establishment of a relationship between Korean culture and foreign culture reflected both a reality and the government's propaganda from the time of the emergence of the Park regime; all evils in the society came from unquestioning acceptance of foreign cultures, including remnants of colonial rule, and so South Koreans should unite with their own culture as the centre. This rhetoric was basically for political propaganda. However, its influence was also powerful in arousing the ethnic national sensitivity of the South Korean public in the field of culture.

In this context, the following remarks show what response the government and NMK wanted to get from the public. *Bangmulgwan shinmun* introduced the following comment of an attendee at the Culture Lecture for Teenagers, which was launched by NMK in August 1984, and clearly showed how and why NMK approached the public:

> I feel proud as a Korean anew; I fully realised that we should succeed to and develop our traditional culture; I feel proud to understand our [culture] and have got to attain self-sovereignty; I feel liberated from our inferiority complex, and I am thankful to my ancestors.[29]

It can be said that this comment was the "correct answer" that the government wanted from the public. In other words, education programmes at NMK were intended to unite Korean nationals by cultivating in them a strong consciousness of ethnic nationalism.

Reopening of NMK in the former building of the Government-General

The reopening of NMK in the former building of the Government-General on 21 August 1986 gave NMK an opportunity to renovate its galleries and expand its educational functions. The total area of the galleries doubled, from 4,890m² to 9,871m². Furthermore, the number of exhibits more than tripled, from 2,300 to 7,500 items (Figure 4.1). In March 1986, NMK summarised the main purpose of its permanent exhibition as follows:

> providing the South Korean nationals and foreigners with an understanding of Korean ethnic national culture's legitimacy and its developmental system from a cultural historical perspective, and helping them view the characteristics and superiority of Korean arts, as well as contributing to comparative research on the surrounding culture.[30]

According to this purpose, NMK professed itself to be both art museum and history museum, as shown through new permanent galleries, emphasising that NMK should be worthy of its name: literally the national central museum. This objective was to be accomplished by placing importance on national education, the main task of which was to make nationals take pride in their ethnic national culture.[31] In this regard, NMK tried to compile in the new permanent galleries all the academic accomplishments since the liberation. First of all, the "developmental system" of Korean ethnic national culture was reconstructed according to time periods. The first floor of the museum covered periods from prehistory to Unified Silla, exhibiting archaeological artefacts. Especially, all the phases of prehistoric age were reorganised from the Palaeolithic Age to the Early Iron Age, suggesting the Korean ethnic nation's long history.

A gallery for the Proto-Three Kingdoms period was newly established in order to prove the independent formation of early states whose cultural basis had been on early ironware culture in the Korean peninsula.[32] This reorganisation of Korean ancient history was instrumental in denying the Japanese colonial perspective on Korean history. The Gaya confederation (42–562, fourth political entity of the Three Kingdoms period, whose history was not clear in the historical document), got to have its own gallery in the new building. Reconstructing the history of Gaya, which was located in the southern area of the peninsula, between the Baekche Kingdom (18 BCE–660 CE) and the Silla Kingdom (57 BCE–935), had a special meaning for denying the argument made during the colonial period that Japanese had occupied the territory of Gaya in the 6th century.

The second floor included galleries of ceramics and metal craft from the Goryeo period to the Joseon period, as well as galleries for donated artefacts. Also on this floor was the opening of a scholar's studio or sarangbang. This studio, a reproduction of an equivalent building in the late Joseon period, symbolised the reinstatement of the culture of the period, which had been ignored as stagnant and dependant by the Japanese colonial view. Just as the Japanese traditional tea room was branded and introduced to the West as a typical image of Japanese culture, so this sarangbang would play

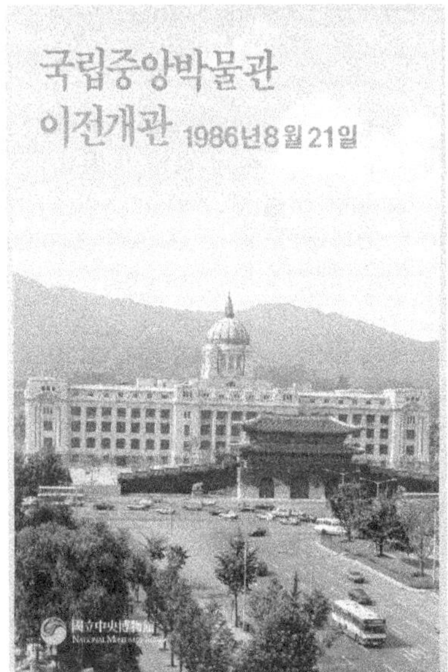

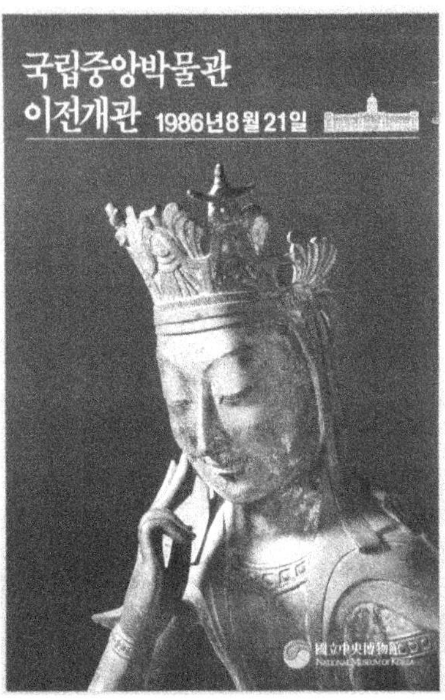

Figure 4.1 Posters in commemoration of the reopening of the National Museum of Korea in the former Government-General building in August 1986. With kind permission from NMK.

the same role for Koreans from this time forward.[33] This sarangbang was intended for displaying an elegant and graceful aspect of the literati of the Joseon dynasty.[34]

The third floor included newly established galleries for foreign cultures, including Chinese culture and Japanese culture. In these galleries, NMK secured space for its special collections: a Central Asian collection (the so-called Ottani collection); a Sin-an shipwreck collection excavated off the south-western shore of Korea in the 1970s; and the Nangnang collection, which was excavated by Japanese scholars during the colonial period. The culture of the Nangnang was intended to be considered as a foreign culture transplanted from China, not the origin of Korean ancient culture. It is worth noting that, on this floor, NMK established a gallery for Korean Buddhist paintings, which, from the late 1960s, began to draw attention as being among the great accomplishments of Korean painting. This new permanent exhibition reflected the outcomes that the South Korean academics had accumulated since the liberation, and also meant the completion of the ethnic nationalist narrative through material culture. At his address on the reopening, Director Han Byeong-sam (in office from 1984 to 1993) commented, "NMK came to have an appearance as place for social education in which to view and feel our five thousand year long culture more systematically and tridimensionally."[35]

The concept of social education had double meanings in the contemporary context. In the Law of Social Education, enacted on 31 December 1982, social education was defined as all forms of organisational education activities for life-long education for the nationals except regular schooling, and the museum and library were included as such organisations for social education.[36] This law provided that the purpose of social education was to improve the calibre of citizens and, by doing so, to make them contribute to the development of their country and society. Under pressure for the democratisation of South Korean society, the government adopted the concept of life-long education as a dispensation towards nationals even in the constitution revised in 1981. However, its ultimate orientation was for encouraging the people to contribute to the country by following the government's leadership.

This point gets clearer in President Chun's message in 1986.[37] He put emphasis on avoiding the split in national opinion and maintaining national unity. His remark was one of his solutions to people's antipathy towards his regime. As Eckert (1990a, p. 378) says, the Gwangju uprising continued to haunt Chun. He persisted in President Park's repressive policies, with only a few superficial changes. Demand for political freedom and economic equity continued to increase, and the regime would ultimately resort to the national police force. It was in this context that Lee Won-hong, the minister of Culture and Information, reported to Chun on the projects of the year 1986 that the ministry should strengthen public communication so that the government could lead the way in correcting the consciousness, logic and attitude of nationals, thereby laying the foundation of national harmony and participating in the formation of public opinion.[38] Lee reported that the ministry would strengthen the social educational function of museums for broadening the foundation on which to cultivate "independent culture."

As ever, the rhetoric of the cultivation of independent culture was intended as a medium of national unity by the government. However, South Korean society was changing somewhat. Contributions to *Bangmulgwan shinmun* for commemorating the reopening of NMK in 1986 showed that South Korean intellectuals were conscious of such changes, even though they were also thought to hold quite a firm ethnic nationalist stance. Lee Gu-yeol, a journalist who specialised in the cultural sector, mentioned that the museum should be opened to the public so that anyone could be familiar with it without feeling pressured. He added that the museum should be a pleasant and free space where people of all social groups could visit and be impressed.[39] Kim Byeong-mo, a professor at Hanyang University, urged that the museum should thoughtfully consider every detail, from explanatory labels to chairs for visitors, so that all visitors could enjoy the museum.[40] Lee Gyeong-seong, director of the National Museum of Contemporary Art, also emphasised the importance of educational outcomes, insisting that the museum should be a space for education through cultural objects, not a place for them to gather dust. He recommended expansion of lecture programmes and educational facilities, including video rooms.[41]

Social education after reopening in 1986

As suggested in Director Han's address on the reopening of NMK in 1986, NMK focused on the museum education programmes after the reopening. In accordance with the reopening in the former capitol building, NMK secured an annex building for social education which was 4,922m^2 of the total floor space. The Section for Cultural Education was established in order to take full control of the related business. In addition to these ongoing programmes, NMK added new education programmes. The first was the Saturday Open Lectures, beginning on 6 September, right after the reopening (NMK, 2006, p. 261). This programme was intended for employees who were finding it difficult to make time for their studies. The course covered art history, archaeology, history, folklore and anthropology.

In *Bangmulgwan shinmun* in December 1986, NMK published its education programmes for the following year, listing them one by one.[42] On the basis of the facility's infrastructure and organisation, in 1987 NMK began to push forward various education programmes. NMK explained the purpose and vision of the programmes:

> NMK is working on diverse social education programmes in order to provide nationals in general with changes in lifelong education, and to instil cultural consciousness into them through correct understandings of our indigenous tradition and history. These programmes are in accordance with the needs of the times that the museum should not remain a store of artefacts, but become a guide for the development of national and local culture.[43]

NMK launched two more new education programmes in 1987, for the elderly and children, respectively. The former, Museum School for the Elderly, was intended for an older demographic, those who "have lived their life during turbulent eras, such as colonial rule and the Korean War." NMK explained that the purpose of this programme was "for making the elderly recognise the superiority of our traditional culture and gain a correct understanding of Korean history, and by doing so, for correcting their distorted values and perspective on history." The other programme, Museum Class for Children, was run during the children's summer and winter vacations, just like the Museum Class for Teenagers, which made its start in 1984.

The year 1987 was a turning point in the democratisation of South Korea. As Eckert (1990a, p. 382) says, President Chun had to accept quite reformative proposals from his fellow conspirator of the 1979 coup, Roh Tae-woo (Born in 1932), who would be a candidate for the next presidency from 1988. The proposals included a direct presidential election and restoration of civil rights for Kim Dae-jung, a strong opposition leader. This stream of democratisation in the 1980s allowed the public to have more chance of access to the national museum.

The ambiguous expression "cultural consciousness" is interesting, especially alongside the rhetoric used regarding the Museum School for the Elderly. It is thought to have meant a high level of consciousness which could only be achieved by national pride in the cultural accomplishments of the Korean ethnic nation. This expression could be said to imply that NMK had no difficulty in continuing to utilise this ethnic nationalist rhetoric for national unity in order to explain the purpose of its activities, despite the aversion of society to state violence in this period. It seems that democratisation helped the South Korean public to absorb an ethnic nationalist consciousness through widened opportunities to access their material culture. It means that South Korean public could internalise the ethnic nationalist consciousness through their material culture more voluntarily. Indeed, the ethnic nationalist rhetoric developed by the government since Park Chung Hee's regime can be said to have become a firm foundation of such internalisation.

In the commemorative speech given by the minister of Culture and Information at the ground-breaking ceremony for the construction of Jeonju National Museum, a new branch museum of NMK was introduced:

> the construction of this museum means that both the government and nationals have the same willingness to correctly inherit and develop the ethnic cultural heritage in accordance with the mood in which recognition of our cultural creative capability and its autonomy is increasingly improving.[44]

His remark clearly reflects a mood of democratisation, and also shows that he was confident in maintaining the discourse of ethnic national culture in a changing South Korean society. In the same context, one of the staff members, in his contribution to *Bangmulgwan shinmun*, concluded that the Museum Special Lectures programme achieved the expected outcomes, arguing that the attendees had a unanimous opinion that these lectures helped them to understand their culture and history, which they had not hitherto known, and did not have pride in or affection for.[45]

It is noteworthy, however, that South Korean intellectuals who resisted the authoritarian leaders and their policies also had a strong ethnic nationalist orientation. Given that they criticised the leaders' dictatorships or humiliating diplomatic policies towards the US or Japan, they were clearly against these regime and foreign powers; it is also clear that they had an ethnic nationalist perspective, even though that perspective could be differentiated from official ethnic nationalism driven by the government. As Hong points out, their perspective had the high possibility of being absorbed into the government's discourse on the ethnic nationalism (Hong, 2002, pp. 197–8). The field of Korean history and material culture was one of the representative fields.

Special exhibitions held by NMK between 1986 and 1995 showed a characteristic trend. As shown in Kang Woo-bang's (the then chief curator of art history at NMK) argument that special exhibitions should concretely present several aspects of Korean art history one by one,[46] special exhibitions in this period began to have a clear sense of subject. *Masterpieces of Celadon of the Goryeo Period* (1989), *Woodcraft of the Joseon Period* (1989), *Buddhist Sculpture in the Three Kingdoms Period* (1990), *Buddhist Reliquary* (1991), *Paintings of Gyeomjae Jeong Son* (1992), *Korean Arts of the 18th Century* (1993) and *Paintings of Danwon* (1995) are just a few examples. Pressing issues relating to prehistory and ancient history were also dealt with in archaeological special exhibitions: *Culture of Gaya Kingdom* (1991), *Bronzeware Culture of Korea* (1992) and *Prehistoric and Proto-historic Earthenware* (1993) (NMK, 2006, p. 216). These exhibitions were intended to display independent cultural development throughout the Korean peninsula.

When NMK reopened in August 1986, it could expand and also add convenient facilities, such as a parking lot and dining areas, aiming to attract more visitors. NMK attempted to provide visitors with teaching materials for each gallery from May 1988.[47] From April 1989, NMK allowed free entry for children and teenagers below 18 years of age and for the elderly above 65 years of age.[48] The Ministry of Culture established in January 1990 anticipated a transition in cultural policy. Its first minister, Lee Eo-ryeong, who had been a professor at Ewha Womans' University and a cultural critic, promised to discard bureaucratic customs and centralism from the cultural administration (Park, 2010, pp. 164–6). One of the major objectives of the ministry in 1990 was the expansion of nationals' right to enjoy culture and participate in it.[49]

This persistent promotion of ethnic national culture by the government, and the resulting spread of ethnic national sensitivity in South Korean society, were finally proved by a cultural "incident." Remarkably, in 1993 this society encountered its first best-seller on the cultural heritage of Korea. *Naui munhwayusan dapsagi* [My Essay on the Exploration of Cultural Heritage], written by Yu Hong-jun (born in1949), was recorded as the sixth best-selling book in that year, becoming the first ever million-seller in the field of liberal arts publications in South Korea. As shown in his first expression in the book, "our country's territory is all a museum," Yu, an art historian and art critic, showed that he was proud that he could encounter both tangible and intangible heritage wherever he went in the country. He added:

> Our country has a very small territory; however, our country has a very rare experience in which one ethnic nation lived that long history in the same area as a community bound together by a common destiny, maintaining the same blood, language, institutions and customs.
>
> (Yu, 1993, pp. 5–7)

In the preface to his book, Yu also lamented that Koreans failed to read the truth about and learn of the beauty of the artefacts from the national territory, falling instead into hopeless envy and imitation of others' cultures. He continued to explain why he authored the book: "I, as a guide of the museum, wanted to share my happiness by which to embrace the history and aesthetics of the national territory with all the people living with me in the same period" (Yu, 1993, pp. 5–7). His understanding exactly followed director Choi Sunu's, although Yu had a background as an anti-government intellectual, who had fought against Park Chung Hee's dictatorship.[50] This is a good example that shows that another stream of nationalism in South Korean society, an anti-thesis to official nationalism by the government, still shared almost the same ethnic national sensitivity in terms of their material culture (Hong, 2002, pp. 191–198).

From 1985 he participated, as a co-chairman in the Council of Ethnic National Art, whose aim was to promote the movement *Minjung misul* [Art for Those Who Are Ruled]. He became a lecturer at a private university in a local city in 1991, before taking the lead in a cultural movement exploring cultural remains, lecturing university students on Korean art history and contributing essays on explorations to *Jugan hanguk*.[51] Responses to the book were very enthusiastic, as the record sales show. In her contribution to *The Kyunghyangshinmun*, Park Wan-seo (1931–2011), a famous South Korean novelist, highly praised Yu's book, saying, "I am so pleased to read this book and realise very much that I cannot help talking about it." She added:

> While reading this book, I experienced a surprise as if a blind person opened one's eyes. When I was a middle school student, I faced

> liberation [from the Japanese colonial rule]. It was natural to put emphasis on teaching the superiority of our ethnic national culture in order to recover our self-respect which had miserably been stamped down. So I repeatedly had to hear the expressions, 'five thousand years' long history' and 'our brilliant culture.' … I just learned about them only through textbooks without exploring [cultural remains], and experienced the Korean War. It was not before we put all our ethnic national energy into how to earn a living and how to survive that we got into the condition to enjoy culture, and began to have an interest in cultural heritage. This change took place around the early 1970s, as my first visit to Gyeongju in that period shows. However, I was disappointed that Bulguksa temple and Seokguram grotto were not that brilliant. … I did not know how to express to what extent I was shocked to visit the British Museum and the Louvre Museum. Seeing so many brilliant things there, I felt betrayed, and experienced a sense of inferiority in terms of ours on which I heard only blind praise. … The shock left a long lasting hurt to me, and an attempt to soothe the hurt might arouse a motivation to appreciate ours.[52]

Through her personal experiences, Park exactly described how South Korean nationals had approached and recognised their material culture for the past 50 years, as well as why this book had been such a success. The South Korean public were taught to have pride in their national material culture through promotion policy by the government. However, pride would only follow after they were able to enjoy culture and appreciate their ethnic national culture on their own. As it was, they were hurt by the gap between what they actually felt about their cultural heritage and what that cultural heritage was supposed to be.

As Park mentioned, this gap can be said to have taken place because the South Korean public were forced to have pride in their culture without having the opportunity to appreciate and enjoy it. Yu's book attempted to present the public with a way to view and appreciate cultural heritages, which was a decisive factor in its great success. He effectively aroused ethnic national sensitivity from the cultural heritage about which he wrote, providing readers with abundant information with which to understand their cultural heritage. Yu has continued to publish a series of follow-ups on his exploration of the subject, achieving the record of selling three million books in the 20 years since the publication of the first book. In 1997, a part of his book was even inserted in a textbook of Korean language-learning for middle school students. Furthermore, his book was chosen as the second most important book of the 1990s by a major bookstore on the recommendation of a committee comprising 18 intellectuals.[53]

His success shows that South Korean society began to have a popular groundswell for appreciating material culture in the early 1990s. It should not be overlooked that this was also a product of the dissemination policy of the discourse on ethnic national culture by the government, even though Yu was against the authoritarian regimes. It is in this context that the South Korean public was also eager to understand their material culture as ethnic culture. Yu was also a faithful follower of this tendency, and this factor clearly gave him great success.

Demolition of the building of NMK and the "righteous spirit of the ethnic nation"

The authoritarian decision by President Chun to reopen NMK in the former building of the Government-General was followed by controversy. Within four years of the reopening, opinions on the relocation or demolition of the building of NMK were raised in a democratic mood in South Korean society after the success of the pro-democracy movement and the revision of the constitution, which had led to the revival of the system of direct election in the presidential election of December 1987. The new president, Rho Tae-woo (in office from 1988 to 1993), could not help but accede to demands for democratisation, taking several actions to complement his legitimacy. One of the actions was the restoration of Gyeongbokgung Palace, the primary royal palace of the Joseon dynasty, most of whose buildings were demolished (except for the main buildings in the centre zone) during colonial rule. The demolition was symbolised by the erection of the Government-General building in 1926 on the site secured by the demolition of the southern zone of the palace.

This palace restoration project, which also became one of the projects commemorating the 600 years since the founding of the capital in Seoul in 1394, accrued diverse meanings – including even democratisation – because its restoration needed the relocation of the security force compound for the presidential residence, *Cheogwadae*.[54] However, the most important cause for the project soon became the elimination of the colonial remnants.[55] In this regard, the palace began to be believed to symbolise the historical legitimacy of the Korean ethnic nation. This belief gradually became prevalent in the vortex of controversy over the issue of the demolition of the Government General building. The press also contributed to the diffusion of this belief by introducing contributions from historians to general readers which mostly supported the demolition of the building,[56] while some newspapers tried to be neutral.[57]

On 1 April 1993, President Kim Young-sam (in office from 1993 to 1997) finally decided to demolish the former building of the Government-General that was being occupied by NMK. Kim, who had long been a leader of the opposition party, had become president through a coalition with the ruling party, whose main members were related to the military coup in 1979. He took pride in being the first president who did not have any military background since the coup by Park Chung Hee. However, he was criticised for entering a coalition with the former ruling clique that had staged the military coup, even though he strove to differentiate himself from them and had a strong background as a fighter for democracy. It seems that this might be one of the reasons why he was eager to claim that he would eliminate the colonial remnants in South Korean society. This task became one of the most important and urgent items on his to-do list. Within a month of assuming office, President Kim gave the order to demolish the building and relocate NMK. His decision was made only seven years after NMK was relocated in the building in 1986.

His decision aroused immediate controversy in South Korean society. While some intellectuals objected to the decision for several reasons, *The Dong-AIlbo* supported his decision.[58] This controversy reached a climax when the demolition began in August 1995. Even the ruling party was worried about public opinion and asked the president to put off the demolition, because the planned relocation of NMK was still uncertain.[59] However, President Kim was adamant about demolishing the building. And it seems that the government desperately needed a symbolic event for commemorating the 50th anniversary of the liberation, so decided to proceed with demolishing the building on 15 August 1995. The main event of the ceremony marking the anniversary was the demolition of the steeple over the dome of the building. The minister of Culture and Sports made a speech, saying:

> by demolishing the building of the Government General, which obliterated our ethnic nation's language and history and even deprived us of our rights to live, I solemnly swear to liquidate the gloomy past and revive the righteous spirit of our ethnic nation through the restoration project of Gyeongbokgung Palace.[60]

The demolition project resumed in July 1996, as a temporary space for NMK had to be secured before the demolition began.[61] The project was not finished until the end of the year. NMK reopened at the renovated annex building, which had been utilised for social education, on 12 December 1996. This controversial issue over the demolition clearly showed how the ethnic national sensitivity could have a tremendous influence on South Korean society, especially when the issue was related to Japanese colonial rule. Despite the increasing interest in cultural objects in the 1990s, it did not seem that the national museum could have its own voice in the vortex of this controversy.

"Grand" opening of NMK in 2005

On 31 October 1997, in his address at the ground-breaking ceremony for the new NMK building, President Kim Young-sam anticipated that the museum would be a superb cultural space to accommodate the self-respect and pride of the Korean ethnic nation. He added that this museum would contribute to firmly establishing the subjectivity of the ethnic nation in the era of globalisation and unification. Furthermore, he said that all of these efforts were for heightening the righteous spirit of the ethnic nation and correcting the history which had been distorted.[62] Like his predecessors, he intended to fully utilise the ethnic national sentiment in South Korean society. His comments reveal the extent to which the rhetoric of ethnic national culture took hold in Korea.

In the 1990s, South Korean society experienced a spirit of democratisation. As discussed earlier in this chapter, Kim Young-sam, an opposition party leader with no military background, was elected president in December 1992, despite criticism for entering the coalition with the former ruling clique who had staged the military coup. As Cumings points out, in November 1995, President Kim Young-sam displayed the progress of democracy in South Korea by jailing two former presidents, Chun Doo-hwan and Roh Tae-woo, for the military coup in 1979 and for the bloody suppression of the civilian uprising in Gwangju in 1980, respectively (Cumings, 2005, p. 395). The election of Kim Dae-jung as president in December 1997, another opposition party leader and lifelong fighter for democracy, showed that "Korea's civil society and democracy were both strong and vibrant, and no longer threatened by the military," as Cumings (2005, p. 400) argues. Kim Dae-jung (in office from 1993 to 1998) supported Roh Moo-hyun to succeed him in office in the next presidential election in December 2002. Roh was a lawyer who, in the 1980s, had defended many dissidents and labour activists. By his winning the election, Kim Dae-jung and Roh Moo-hyun achieved a thorough political transition away from the elites who had dominated South Korea since 1948 (Cumings, 2005, pp. 400–1).

The 12-year-long grand project of constructing the new museum building finally reached its fruition on 28 October 2005. As shown above, President Roh Moo-hyun's address at the opening ceremony reflected another stream of Korean ethnic nationalism which tended to be against authoritarian regimes and foreign powers. From his perspective, he was treading the right path of ethnic nationalism, while the former authoritarian regimes were not considered to have done so. Interestingly, however, both sides appealed to the ethnic nationalist sentiment implied by the national museum. This shows to what extent ethnic nationalism and its representation through material culture was important in South Korean society, as before it had been under the control of authoritarian regimes. In this regard, it can be also understood that material culture did become one of the essential mediums that could represent and prove nationhood (Figure 4.2).

With the opening of the new building, the total area of the galleries expanded from 9,871m^2 to 27,090m^2. Aiming for an audience-friendly museum and a complex cultural space, NMK prided itself in its newly furnished children's museum, expanded education programmes, convenient facilities and digital devices for guidance, as well as a large-scale performance hall and auditoriums. Permanent exhibitions were classified under four headings: history, fine arts, gifts and Asian arts. Remarkably, NMK first adopted the name of Asian Arts Galleries, although the museum had already established Chinese, Japanese and Central Asian galleries in 1986. NMK included an Indonesian Art gallery, with exhibits loaned by the Jakarta National Museum of Indonesia. NMK explained the establishment of the gallery as being for "giving the viewers a chance to understand the commonality and diversity of Asia and to experience characteristics of each culture." Interestingly, NMK saw the establishment of the gallery as a means to become one of Asia's most important museums.[63] This implied that the gallery was, in part, intended for a national ambition as well as for understanding its culture.

The archaeological gallery newly included a section devoted to the Balhae kingdom (698–926), whose founder was a former general of Goguryeo, one of the Three Kingdoms. Almost all South Korean historians

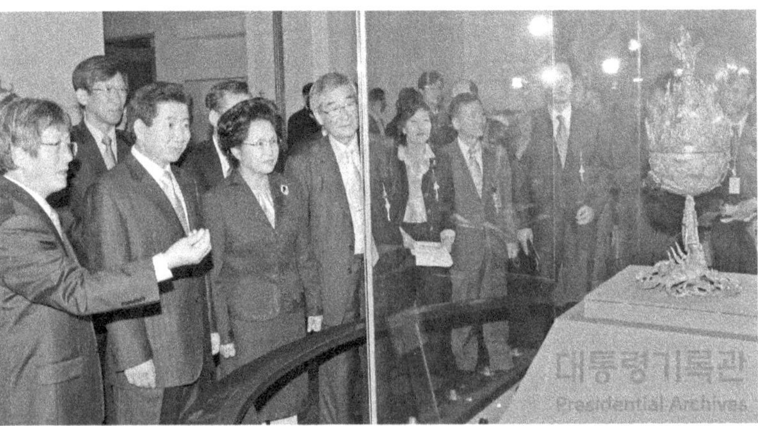

Figure 4.2 President Roh Moo-hyun at the reopening ceremony of the National Museum of Korea in October 2005. With kind permission from the National Archives of Korea.

have not hesitated to view this kingdom as a part of Korean national history, since the kingdom was argued to be one of the ancient countries of Korean history in the late 18th century;[64] while the Chinese historical circle urged that the kingdom and even the Goguryeo kingdom were local regimes in Chinese history.[65] Against the Chinese side's argument, NMK took an active part in presenting material evidence in support of the argument from the Korean side by the establishment of this section of the gallery. This can be considered to have been an attempt to prove the discourse on national history through museum activity. Expectations of perfection of the discourse came from the South Korean audience. The museum involved an event involving a chronological table displayed in the archaeological gallery. Some audience members complained to the museum about the fact that the table did not include Gojoseon, the first country in the history of Korea. This issue attracted the attention of the press.[66] Finally, the museum could not help acceding to demands from the public and press. This issue shows to what extent the South Korean public and press internalised the nationalist discourse on history. In addition, it was a good example of how the national museum responded to a nationalist demand from the public.

In August 2010, NMK finished the renovation of the history gallery, which was directed by the then director Choe Gwang-sik (in office from 2008 to 2011). In his preface to an exhibition catalogue, Choe summarised the renovation as for the construction of "a building with a thread of connection in Korean history."[67] With the renovation, he established a gallery for each dynasty, such as the Goryeo and Joseon dynasties. In other words, his ultimate goal was to show the audiences the whole history of the nation of Korea in the national museum more chronologically and systematically. He was proud that with this renovation, NMK got to have a gallery for every dynasty, from Gojoseon, the first state in Korean history, to the Joseon dynasty. The next director, Kim Youngna (in office from 2011 to 2016), asserted that the permanent exhibitions of NMK are intended to serve as extensions of the national history textbooks, and that the narrative they provide is within the bounds of official history (Kim, 2015, pp. 10–1). It seems that her comment is based on the chronological setting of the history gallery, which was renovated in 2010.

Most mass media's positive appraisal of the renovation showed to what extent South Korean society has internalised the nationalistic perspective on the interpretation of material culture and its history.[68] Although Duara argues that national identity exists only as one among other identities and is changeable, interchangeable, conflicted or harmonious with them (Duara, 1995, p. 8), there does not seem to be enough space for other identities to be secured in the arena of the national museum. It is difficult to say that issues of gender, ethnicity, class and centre-province relations are actively discussed in the exhibitions of NMK. For example, the literati class of the Joseon dynasty is focused on only as a bearer of high culture, even though it definitely had a more complex socio-economical background and context in its contemporary society. In the same context, it is not easy to find discussions of gender issues or centre-province relations in NMK's exhibitions.

Notes

1 NMK, *Bangmulgwan nyuus* [The Museum News], vol.2, 1 August 1970, p. 4.
2 Ibid., vol.5, 1 November 1970, p. 1 and vol.12, 1 June 1971, p. 1.
3 *Bangmulgwan shinmun*, vol.22, 1 May 1972, p. 1.
4 Ibid., vol.34, 1 December 1973, p. 1.
5 Ibid., vol.28, 1 June 1973, p. 3.
6 Ibid., vol.44, 1 November 1974, p. 4.
7 Ibid., vol. 42, 1 August 1974, p. 1 & vol.37, 1 March 1974, p. 2.
8 Ibid., vol.28, 1 June 1973, p. 1.
9 Ibid., vol.43, 1 September 1974, p. 3.
10 Choi Sunu, "Bangmulgwan ui baljeon [The Development of the Museum]," ibid., vol.37, 1 March 1974, p. 1.
11 Ibid., vol.34, 1 September 1973, p. 1.
12 Ibid., vol.47, 1 March 1975, p. 1. See also ibid., vol.56, 1 March 1976, p. 4.
13 Ibid., vol. 55, February 1976, p. 4.
14 Ibid., vol.45, 1 January 1975, p. 1.
15 Ibid., vol.25, 1 January 1973, p. 4.
16 Ibid., vol. 93, 1 May 1979, p. 4.
17 Furthermore, the new constitution added a phrase, the "promotion of ethnic national culture" to the swearing in of the new president.
18 Park Seok-heung, "Je 5 gonghwaguk munhwajeongchak ui banghyang gwa eui [The Significance and Direction of the Cultural Policy of the Fifth Republic: Laying the Foundation for the Ethnic National Culture]," *The Kyunghyang shinmun*, 23 June 1981.
19 "Gungnip jungang bangmulgwan ijeonhwakjang gyehoekbalpyo [The Statement of the Relocation and Expansion Plan of the National Museum of Korea]," *Bangmulgwan shinmun*, vol.128, 1 April 1982, p. 1.
20 "Gwacheon cheongsaro ijeon [The Relocation of Several Government Ministries, Such as the Ministry of Law, into the Gwacheon]," *The Dong-A Ilbo*, 16 March 1982.
21 "Yeongyok ui hyeonjang eul yeongwonhan minjok ui gyohuneuro [From the Site of Shame and Glory into the Eternal Lesson of the Ethnic Nation]," *The Kyunghyang Shinmun*, 16 March 1982.
22 *The Kyunghyang Shinmun*, 27 May 1981.
23 *Hangukgyeongje shinmun*, 28 February 1981.
24 *The Dong-A Ilbo*, 30 March 1981.
25 *The Kyunghyang Shinmun*,12 December 1981.
26 *Bangmulgwan shinmun*, vol.69, 1 April 1977, p. 1.
27 Song Jeong-suk, "Munhwa ui heogitjeung [Hunger for Culture]," ibid., vol.119, 1 July 1981, p. 4.
28 Choi Jin-yong, "Bangmulgwan hwaldong e geoneun gidae [Expectation towards Museum Activities]," ibid., vol.93, 1 May 1979, p. 4.

29 Ibid., vol.157, 1 September 1984, p. 1.
30 "Gungnip jungang bangmulgwan ijeongaegwan annae [Notice of the Relocation and Reopening of NMK]," ibid., vol.175, 31 March 1986, p. 1.
31 Ibid.
32 "Jinyeolsil annae: wonsamguksil [Introducing Galleries: Proto Three Kingdom]," ibid., vol.184, 31 December 1986, p. 2.
33 The British Museum included this studio in its permanent galley of Korean culture in 1990. See K. Kim, *Korea As Seen through Its Material Culture and Museums*, Unpublished PhD thesis, University of Leicester, 2005, pp. 269–71. For the role of tea in making Japanese identity, see Surak, 2013.
34 *Bangmulgwan shinmun*, vol.193, 1 September 1987, pp. 3–4.
35 Han Byeong-sam, "Uri munhwa baljeon ui sae jeongi [A Turning Point of Development of Our Culture]," ibid., vol.180, 21 August 1986, p. 1.
36 Available at: http://www.law.go.kr/lsInfoP.do?lsiSeq=2892&ancYd=19821231&ancNo=03648&efYd=19830701&nwJoYnInfo=N&efGubun=Y&chrClsCd=010202#0000. Accessed 16 February 2019.
37 *Bangmulgwan shinmun*, vol.174, 28 February 1986, p. 1.
38 Ibid.
39 Ibid., vol.180, 21 August 1986, p. 5.
40 Ibid.
41 Ibid.
42 Ibid., vol.184, 31 December 1986, p. 1.
43 Ibid., vol.187, 31 March 1987, p. 1.
44 Ibid., vol.197, 31 January 1988, p. 1.
45 Ibid., vol.191, 31 July 1987, p. 3.
46 Ibid., vol.180, 31 August 1986, p. 4.
47 Ibid., vol.201, 31 May 1988, p. 4.
48 Ibid., vol.212, 30 April 1989, p. 1.
49 Ibid., vol.222, 28 February 1990, p. 1.
50 In 1967, he was admitted into the Department of Aesthetics at Seoul National University. He was suspended from the school for his participation in a protest against the revision of the constitution during President Park Chung Hee's third term. In 1974, he was involved in an infamous fabricated incident of espionage and imprisoned. He was freed in February 1975 and worked for art-related journals during the second half of the 1970s. See "Seokhak ege deutnunda: Yu hong-jun myeongjidae gyosu [Interview with Professor Yu Hong-jun]," *Jugan hanguk* [Weekly Korea], 16 October 2003.
51 Ibid.
52 Park Wan-seo, "Naneun gieoi malhago sipdda [I Necessarily Like to Say]," *The Kyunghyang Shinmun*, 27 July 1993.
53 *The Kyunghyang Shinmun*, 2 December 1999.
54 Anon, "Gyeongbokgung yet moseup doe channeunda [Gyeongbokgung Palace Regains Its Former Images],' *Hankyoreh shinmun* [The Hankyoreh]," 20 September 1988.
55 On 27 October 1989, at a symposium held by the Culture and Art Promotion Centre, a government-sponsored research institution, Professor Cho Heung-yun of Hanyang University in Seoul argued that the Gyeongbokgung Palace should be restored in order to regain the subjectivity of the ethnic nation and eliminate remnants of colonial rule. See Lee Yong-u, 'Gwan ipgim julyeoya minganmunhwa baljeon [Less Intervention from the Government Leads to Development of

Civilian Culture],' *The Dong-A Ilbo*, 28 October 1989; Kim Cha-su, 'Ilje janjae ui sangjing dugoman bwayahana [Should We Just Maintain and See the Symbol of the Colonial Remnant?]' *The Dong-A Ilbo*, 6 December 1990.

56 In 1990, most major South Korean newspapers included contributions from readers and academics. For example, *The Dong-A Ilbo*, 5 August 1990; *The Kyunghyang Shinmun*, 2 November 1990; *Hankyoreh shinmun*, 13 November 1990.

57 These newspapers introduced the pros and cons of the issue. See *Hankyoreh shinmun* (6 November 1990) and *The Dong-A Ilbo* (4 December 1990).

58 "Joseon chongdokbu geonmul gwa gukmin jajonsim [The Building of Government-General and the Nationals' Self-Respect]," *The Dong-A Ilbo*, 3 April 1993.

59 "Yet chongdokbu cheolgeo jom chameusijyo [Please Refrain from Demolishing the Building]," *Hankyoreh shinmun*, 1 August 1995.

60 *Bangmulgwan shinmun*, vol.289, 30 September 1995, p. 1.

61 "Gu chongdokbu geonmul 7 wol bongyeok cheolgeo [The Demolition of the Building of Government-General Begins in July]," *The Dong-A Ilbo*, 9 April 1996, p. 26.

62 "Presidential Address for the Ground-Breaking Ceremony by President Kim Young-sam," 31 October 1997. Available at: http://pa.go.kr/research/contents/speech/index.jsp. Accessed 16 January 2019.

63 A brochure published by NMK for PR concerning the reopening of the museum reads as follows. "The gallery is where the viewers can also sense the rise of the National Museum of Korea as one of Asia's most important museums." See "The Spirit of History, the Power of Culture, the National Museum of Korea," NMK, October 2005.

64 In his book, Yu Deuk-gong (1749-1807) argues that the history of the kingdom should belong to Korean history. See Yu, *Balhaego* [A Research on Balhae], 1784. In modern and contemporary historiography in South Korea, his argument has been widely accepted and included in every history textbook, although a few scholars, such as Lee and Kim, have objected to it. See Lee Jong-wook, *Minjok inga? Gukga inga?* [Ethnic Nation? Or State?], Seoul: Sonamu, 2006, pp. 15–16; Kim Han-gyu, *Hanjung gwangyesa* [The History of the Korean-Chinese Relations], vol.1, Seoul: Arke, 1999, p. 22. Ahn Jeong-bok, one of Yu's contemporaries, also objected to Yu's argument in his book *Dongsa Gangmok* [Annotated Account of Korean History] written in 1758.

65 For the Chinese Northeast Asian Project, see Kim, 2005, pp. 300–17.

66 *The Chosunilbo*, 8 November 2005; *The Dong-A Ilbo*, 16 November 2005; *Hangeorae shinmun*, 28 November 2005.

67 Choe Gwang-sik, "Preface," *Joseon sanong gongsang ui nara* [Joseon, the Country of Scholars, Farmers, Artisans and Tradesmen], Seoul: National Museum of Korea, 2010.

68 *The Chosunilbo* (6 August 2010), *The Munhwa Ilbo* (5 August 2010) and *Yonhap News* (26 July 2010).

Conclusion

The museum and representation of nationhood

Hobsbawm was optimistic about the end of nations and nationalism, concluding that "the owl of Minerva which brings wisdom, said Hegel, flies out at dusk. It is a good sign that it is now circling round nations and nationalism" (Hobsbawm, 1992, p. 192). However, his expectation proved to be hasty, contradicted by the collapse of the Soviet Union and the resulting explosion of nationalism in Eastern European countries (Jang, 2007, pp. 55–6). Furthermore, nationalism in East Asian countries has persistently functioned as a major dynamic influencing the political, economic, social and cultural life in this region. The discussions that have taken place on nations and nationalism include valuations of and perspectives on their influence in the past, present and future. The reason that Smith, a former student of Gellner, who was a representative modernist in nationalism discussions, changed his view to ethno-symbolism and challenged Gellner's modernist view of nationalism was because he could find ethno-symbolic dimensions in terms of the nature of ethnic groups and nations (Gellner, 1999, pp. 31–2; Smith, 2009, pp. 1–2).

In a sense, Smith's approach can be said to have resulted from his decision to search for a sober solution to volatile reality rather than to pursue a vague expectation of applying the cold light of reason. Nationalism is always attractive when it is explained as a cause to compete with and confront others. In this context, ever since the concept of nationalism was introduced into East Asia, it has always been perceived as a positive value, as it was not only a powerful weapon against Western imperialism but also an effective way by which to unite people under the flag of a nation-state and to compete against other nation-states in the region. In Korea, ethnic nationalism has also been a positive value ever since the term was introduced, functioning as an essential ideology in its struggle for independence during the colonial period and for nation building and the nationalisation of South Koreans since the liberation.

This research has focused on the historical, diplomatic and political context in which South Korea is situated. As argued in the preceding chapters, these specific contexts influenced, and often even determined, how and why national identity was pursued by the national museum. First, this research demonstrated that the construction of national identity in building the modern Korean nation-state was closely related to the renewed understanding of the relationship between Korean culture and Chinese culture. It was in this context that NMK strove to find Korean culture's difference and independence from Chinese culture through its material culture. Indeed, drastic changes in Korea's historical perception of China strongly influenced Koreans' perception of Chinese culture. As Eckert (1991, p. 227) argues,

> to exist outside the realm of Chinese culture was, for the Korean elite, to live as a barbarian. … At the beginning of the Yi dynasty, this orientation toward Chinese culture took an official foreign policy called *sadae* or 'serving the great,' where 'the great' of course, meant China.

He adds that "since at least the seventh century the ruling classes in Korea had thought of themselves in cultural terms less as Koreans than as members of a larger cosmopolitan civilization centered on China."

Remarkably, the Japanese imperialist perspective made ill use of this perception of the Korean elite: using it as evidence with which to deny Korea's autonomous capability to create its own culture. It was in this context that Japanese scholars strove to construct the colonial view of Korean history and instil it into Koreans. From the Japanese perspective, Koreans would have to follow and obey a new "great" Japan. Furthermore, the colonial authorities pushed forward the assimilation policy through colonial rule. The Yi Royal Household Museum and the Government-General Museum were utilised in order to prove this Japanese perspective with material evidences. These museums reflected both the political and academic ambitions of the Japanese empire.

In this circumstance, Korean nationalist intellectuals realised that they should make it an essential mission to prove that their culture was "different" from those of the Chinese and Japanese, further discovering the uniqueness and excellence of Korean ethnic culture. It was not until the liberation from colonial rule that the mission became practicable. After the Second World War ended, drastic changes in international politics gave a totally different meaning to the material culture of Korea. US curators and scholars of Asian art wanted to shed new light on the culture of Korea, now liberated from colonial rule. In other words, they were making an attempt to redefine Korean culture as an individual, national culture. This is why the US curators for the first overseas exhibitions in the US were reluctant to include artefacts which showed the strong influence from Chinese culture.

That is, American scholars were also participating in shaping Korean national identity.

From the 1960s, the discourse on ethnic national culture as a political slogan also encouraged the academic circle of Korean historians to challenge the Japanese colonial view of Korean history, and strongly influenced the interpretation of and narratives on Korean material culture. As Korean historians strove to secure evidence of the self-sustainable development of Korean history, NMK made efforts to prove the creativity of Korean culture and its distinctions from Chinese culture. Recognising that the prehistoric age and the Joseon period were the main targets of distortion by Japanese scholars, from the 1960s on the museum focused on investigations of prehistoric relics as well as on rehabilitating the cultural status of the Joseon dynasty.

In this context, Choi Sunu, the fourth director of NMK, asserted that Koreans had built an independent culture and historical foundation as a genuine ethnic nation, and had firmly preserved their beautiful land and language. For him, the museum's urgent task was to help South Korean nationals to understand and appreciate their ethnic national culture. His ambition was accomplished when NMK reopened in August 1986 in the former buildings of both the Government-General and of the South Korean government after the liberation. The findings of this book show how this new National Museum of Korea came to represent the whole of Korean cultural identity through the material culture – an identity that had been constructed by NMK and South Korean academics for the 40 years following 1945. When NMK moved to Yongsan area in Seoul and reopened in 2005, this museum again affirmed the independent cultural identity of the Korean nation. In sum, I believe that this book demonstrates how and why the South Korean government strove and continues to strive to display the uniqueness and independence of Korean culture through the national museum.

Second, this book shows that authoritarian regimes' strong drive to promote national unity drove NMK to establish national identity through material culture. To support his political vision and ambition, Park Chung Hee placed a special emphasis on national unity from the beginning stage of his regime. This 18-year-long regime emphasised strong nationalist policies, one of which was to identify Korean ethnic national culture and promote it. Indeed, he hoped that cultural objects alone were concrete enough evidence to show the possibilities for the reconstruction, innovation and creation of the Korean ethnic nation. Furthermore, he found that ethnic national culture could be a means to mobilise the nationwide cooperation of the populace. In this respect, he repeatedly used evocative vocabulary: "brethren," "forefather" and "fatherland." Indeed, the first word in his inaugural address for his first term as president of South Korea was "Dangun," the sacred progenitor.

In this respect, NMK was an effective government institution through which to put into practice the discourse on ethnic national culture. The expression "ethnic national culture" itself appeared in every corner of the museum. This government-led nationalist drive ensured that the museum collections were considered "ethnic national cultural objects."

The reopening of the museum in a newly erected building in 1972 displayed the government's will to promote the ethnic national culture, and by doing so to secure both the regime's authority and national solidarity with Park's political ambition. His desire for long-term seizure of power resulted in the most systematic dictatorship in the South Korea, through the so-called Revitalisation Constitution promulgated in December 1972. In this regard, he strove to decorate his political ambition in the name of the ethnic nation. This is why some South Korean scholars do not agree that Park was a genuine nationalist but instead redefine his ethnic nationalism as pseudo-ethnic nationalism. In the same context, a South Korean historian even described nationalism in South Korea as being "betrayed" by him (Seo, 2007, pp. 58–75). Nevertheless, Park's promotion of the ethnic national culture, and the resulting dissemination of the discourse on it, did contribute to a revaluation of Korean material culture. Curators at NMK took the lead in uncovering the independent value of Korean culture and building their own authorship, as opposed to the colonial one.

Chun Doo-hwan's authoritarian regime was actually the continuation of Park's regime. He continued to emphasise ethnic national culture, faithfully following Park's ethnic nationalist policies in the cultural sector. After the reopening in the former building of the Government-General in 1986, NMK continued to put forth the ethnic nationalist narrative through its exhibitions and education; the function of education in NMK especially began to be emphasised much more than before. The authoritarian regimes' rhetoric of national identity contributed to the promotion of ethnic national culture. NMK also played an essential role in creating national identity through material culture. This nationalist perspective directed towards Korean ethnic national culture was strongly promoted by the government as well as being supported by academics and national museum curators. Many South Korean academics considered it their urgent mission to construct the South Korean modern nation-state and its national identity, and therefore participated in these government-led projects. Noticeably, South Korean intellectuals who resisted the authoritarian leaders and their policies also had a strong ethnic nationalist orientation, contributing to the dissemination of the discourse on ethnic national culture, as shown in Yu Hong-jun's case. Against this background, the discourse was deeply internalised within South Koreans, increasing South Koreans' interest and pride in their material culture. This internalisation has deeply influenced the formation of South Korean nationalism, as well as of the South Korean modern nation-state.

The political democratisation of South Korean society since 1987 has introduced a more widespread appreciation of material culture. Along with the more systemised nationalist narrative of the national museum, this change gave an easier and more voluntary opportunity for South Koreans to internalise the discourse on their ethnic national culture. The controversy over the demolition of the museum building again aroused a nationalist sentiment. President Kim Young-sam's political utilisation of this sentiment and the people's consent to the demolition made it possible to relocate the national museum in just ten years. The new museum building, which was opened in 2005 in the Yongsan area of Seoul, was steeped in controversy. At the opening ceremony, President Roh Moo-hyun announced that the museum building would stand tall as the focus of the self-respect of the Korean ethnic nation. His remark showed how the government had shaped, and would continue to shape, the museum with regard to Korean nationalism.

Third, it can be argued that international political and diplomatic factors have affected the process of the formation of national identity, although scholars have not paid enough attention to the issue of external factors in terms of the issue of nations and nationalism. After the Second World War ended, NMK, which took over the Government-General Museum right after the liberation in August 1945, soon began to take a step forward in identifying itself as a "national" museum of the South Korean state. South Korea's construction of its own national identity through material culture was also meaningful for furthering US ambition to secure a pro-American regime in the region. In this respect, South Korea's case provides a good example of the ways in which international politics influenced the formation of national identity of a nation which had experienced colonial rule.

As the leading power in the so-called "Free World," the US was eager to teach South Koreans its own civilisation and institutions as the norm that countries under the world order presided over by the US should follow. This American civilisation included museum practice. This is why a major American private foundation, the Rockefeller Foundation, invited Kim Chewon, director of NMK, to the US. His visit gave him confidence in the American standard of museum institutions, and also established, through him, a major gateway through which to transmit Korean cultural resources to the American academic world. The financial assistance from American private foundations such as the Rockefeller Foundation was essential to NMK's conduct of investigation in the 1950s and the 1960s. Likewise, the US was willing to help South Korea find its national identity through material culture.

The overseas touring Korean exhibitions in the US between 1957 and 1959 were representative cultural events that exactly reflected the dynamics of the relationship between South Korea and the US. The US assistance to the South Korean government was essential for national security and the restoration of the damage resulting from the war. These exhibitions showed how material culture could play a practical role in securing the cultural identity and political position of South Korea, impoverished by the war, on the world diplomatic stage. The exhibition also shows that the US was making efforts to ensure that countries under its influence could establish their firm national identity as nation-states. This exhibition also reminded the South Korean government officials of the usefulness and value of material culture and museums.

The second overseas touring exhibition, *5000 Years of Korean Art*, which went to Japan in 1976 and to the US in 1979–1981, was an outcome of both the Park's regime's strong promotion of Korean ethnic culture and NMK's efforts to achieve the recognition of the independent perspectives and the research of South Korean academics. That is, ethnic nationalism became a systematic ideology in South Korea, and all the cultural objects were systematically put in systematic order under the name of the ethnic nation. In this circumstance, NMK and South Korean academics were keen on eliciting favourable responses from American academics and the public on their accomplishments, which they had accumulated for more than 40 years since the liberation. Remarkably, these overseas exhibition projects were embroiled in intense diplomatic issues: between South Korea and Japan and between South Korea and the US. In this regard, these overseas exhibition projects provide a good example of how international cultural exchanges such as exhibitions were utilised for international politics.

This research has traced the trajectory of the National Museum of Korea, focusing on NMK's efforts to construct the national identity through material culture and represent the nationhood of the Korean ethnic nation both at home and abroad. Through this research, it can be argued that since its inauguration in 1945, NMK has undertaken activities for executing national tasks, which include constructing the discourse of ethnic national culture in support of nation building, national unity and internal mobilisation, and securing international recognition of the cultural sovereignty of Korea on the world stage.

References

Ahn, Hwi-jun (1980) *Hanguk hoehwasa* [A History of Korean Paintings], Seoul: Iljisa.

Ahn, Hwi-jun (2000) "Gimjaewon baksa wa gimwonyong gyosu ui misulsajeok giyeo [Art Historical Contributions by Dr. Kim Chewon and Professor Kim Won-yong]," *Misulsa nondan*, 13, pp. 291–304.

Arimitsu, Kyōichi (1985a) "Watashi no chōsen kōkogaku [My Korean Archaeology] (3)," *Kikan sanzenri*, 42, pp. 222–33.

Arimitsu, Kyōichi (1985b) "Watashi no chōsen kōkogaku (4)," *Kikan sanzenri*, 43, pp. 110–21.

Arimitsu, Kyōichi (1985c) "Watashi no chōsen kōkogaku (5)," *Kikan sanzenri*, 44, pp. 194–203.

Armstrong, Charles K. (2003) "The Cultural Cold War in Korea, 1945–1950," *The Journal of Asian Studies*, 62(1), pp. 71–99.

Asian Art Museum of San Francisco (1979) *5000 Years of Korean Art*, San Francisco: Asian Art Museum of San Francisco.

Atkins, E. Taylor (2010) *Primitive Selves: Koreana in the Japanese Colonial Gaze, 1910–1945*, Berkeley: University of California Press.

Balfe, J. H. (1987) "Artworks as Symbols in International Politics," *International Journal of Politics, Culture, and Society*, 1(2), pp. 195–217.

Brazinsky, Gregg (2007) *Nation Building in South Korea: Koreans, Americans, and the Making of a Democracy*, Chapel Hill: University of North Carolina Press.

Caprio, Mark E. (2009) *Japanese Assimilation Policies in Colonial Korea, 1910–1945*, Seattle: University of Washington Press.

Cha, Mun-seong (2008) *Geundae bangmulgwan – geu hyeongseong gwa byeoncheon gwajeong* [Modern Museum: Its Formation and Transition], Paju: Korean Academic Information.

Cha, Sang-cheol (2006) "Iseungman gwa 1950 nyeondae ui hanmi dongmaeng [Rhee Syngman and the Korea-US Alliance in the 1950s]," in Park Jihang et al. (eds.) *Haebang jeonhusa ui jaeinsik* [New Understanding of the History around the Liberation], 2, Seoul: Chagsaesang, pp. 258–92.

Cho, Hui-yeon (2007) *Bakjeonghui wa gaebal dokjae sidae* [Park Chung Hee and His Era of Developmental Dictatorship], Seoul: Yeoksabipyeongsa.

Cho, Hui-yeon (2010) *Dongwondoen geundaehwa* [Mobilised Modernisation], Seoul: Humanitas.

Choe, Gwang-sik (2010) "Preface," in *Sanonggongsang ui nara* [Joseon, the Country of Scholars, Farmers, Artisans and Tradesmen], Seoul: National Museum of Korea.

Choi, Gwang-seung (2012) "Bakjeonghui ui gyeongjugodo gaebalsaeop [Park Chung Hee's Project on Developing the Ancient City]," *Jeongsin munhwa yeongu* [Korean Studies Qurarterly], 35(1), pp. 183–214.

Choi, Sunu (1978) *Hanguk misul ocheonnyeon* [5000 Years of Korean Arts], Seoul: Hyeonamsa.

Chung, Moojeong (2005) "1950 nyeondae miguk e sogaedoen hanguk misul [Korea Art Represented in the US]," *Hanguk geundae misulsahak* [Korean Modern Art History Studies], 14, pp. 7–41.

Clunas, Craig (1997) *Art in China*, Oxford: Oxford University Press.

Cumings, Bruce (2005) *Korea's Place in the Sun: A Modern History*, updated edition, New York and London: W. W. Norton & Company.

Duara, Prasenjit (1995) *Rescuing History from the Nation: Questioning Narratives of Modern China*, Chicago and London: The University of Chicago Press.

Eckert, Carter J. (1990a) "Authoritarianism and Protest, 1948–1990," in C. J. Eckert et al. (eds.) *Korea Old and New: A History*, Seoul: Ilchogak Publishers, pp. 347–87.

Eckert, Carter J. (1990b) "Economic Development in Historical Perspective," in C. J. Eckert et al. (eds.) *Korea Old and New: A History*, Seoul: Ilchogak Publishers, pp. 388–418.

Eckert, Carter J. (1990c) "Liberation, Division, and War," in C. J. Eckert et al. (eds.) *Korea Old and New: A History*, Seoul: Ilchogak Publishers, pp. 327–46.

Eckert, Carter J. (1991) *Offspring of Empire: The Koch'ang Kims and the Colonial Origins of Korean Capitalism*, Seattle and London: University of Washington Press.

Eckert, Carter J. (1999) "Epilogue: Exorcising Hegel's Ghosts: Toward a Postnationalist Historiography of Korea," in Shin Gi-Wook and Michael Robinson (eds.) *Colonial Modernity in Korea*, Cambridge, MA, and London: Harvard University Asia Center, pp. 363–78.

Em, Henry H. (2013) *The Great Enterprise: Sovereignty and Historiography in Modern Korea*, Durham, NC, and London: Duke University Press.

Fujita, Ryosaku (1953) "Chōsen koseki chōsa [Investigation of Korean Historical Remains]," in *Kobunka no hoson to kenkyu* [Preservation and Research of Ancient Cultures], Tokyo: Yoshikawakobunkan, pp. 67–88.

Gang, Hui-jeong (2012) *Nara ui jeonghwa, joseon ui pyosang – iljegangjeomgi seokguram non* [Essence of Nation, Representation of Joseon: A Discussion on Seokguram Grotto], Seoul: Sogang University Press.

Gellner, Ernest (1983[2006]) *Nations and Nationalism*, second edition, Malden: Blackwell Publishing.

Gellner, Ernest (1999) "Adam's Navel: 'Primordialists' Versus 'Modernists'," in Edward Mortimer and Robert Fine (eds.) *People, Nation and State: The Meaning of Ethnicity and Nationalism*, London and New York: I.B. Tauris, pp. 31–5.

Government-General of Korea (1916) *Chōsen hantōsi hensei no yōshi oyobi junjyo* [Essentials and Sequences of Compilation of the History of the Korean Peninsula], Seoul: Government-General of Korea.

Government-General of Korea (1922) *Hutsū gakkō Kokushi – jidōyō* [National History for Primary School Children], Seoul: Government-General of Korea.

Government-General of Korea (1936) *Chōsenshi no shirube* [A Guide to Korean History], Seoul: Government-General of Korea.

Government-General of Korea (1938) *Kodai naisen kankei siryō tokubetsu tenran annai* [A Guide to the Special Exhibition, Relations between Korea and Japan in the Ancient Period], Seoul: Government-General of Korea.

Hahn, Christine Y. (2012) "Unearthing Origins: The Use of Art, Archaeology, and Exhibitions in Creating Korean National Identity, 1945–1962," *Visual Resources: An International Journal of Documentation*, 28(2), pp. 138–70.

Henry, Todd A. (2014) *Assimilating Seoul: Japanese Rule and Politics of Public Space in Colonial Korea, 1910–1945*, Berkeley: University of California Press.

Heo, Eun (2008) *Miguk ui hegemoni wa hanguk minjokjuui* [The US Hegemony and Korean Ethnic Nationalism], Seoul: Minjokmunhwa yeonguso, Korea University.

Hobsbawm, Eric (1983) "Introduction: Inventing Traditions," in Eric Hobsbawm and Terence Ranger (eds.) *The Invention of Tradition*, Cambridge: Cambridge University Press, pp. 1–14.

Hobsbawm, Eric (1992) *Nations and Nationalism Since 1780: Programme, Myth, Reality*, second edition, Cambridge: Cambridge University Press.

Hong, Seok-ryul (2002) "1960 nyeondae hanguk minjokjuui ui du heureum [Two Streams of Korean Ethnic Nationalism in the 1960s]," *Sahoe wa Yeoksa* [Society and History], 62, pp. 169–203.

Hong, Seung-ki (2001) *Hanguk sahaknon* [Discussing the Studies of Korean History], Seoul: Ilchogak.

Horlyck, Charlotte (2013) "Desirable Commodities – Unearthing and Collecting Koryo Celadon Ceramics in the Late Nineteenth and Early Twentieth Centuries," *Bulletin of SOAS*, 76(3), pp. 467–91.

Horlyck, Charlotte and Sascha Priewe (2018) "Displaying a Nation: Representations of Korean Art in the United Kingdom," in Jason Steuber and Allysa B. Peyton (eds.) *Arts of Korea: Histories, Challenges, and Perspectives*, Gainesville: University of Florida Press, pp. 90–115.

Jang, Mun-seok (2007) *Minjokjuui gildeuligi* [Taming Nationalism], Seoul: Jisik ui punggyeong.

Jang, Sang Hoon (2015) *A Representation of Nationhood: The National Museum of Korea*, Unpublished PhD thesis, University of Leicester.

Jang, Sang-hoon (2016) "Cultural Diplomacy, National Identity and National Museum: South Korea's First Overseas Exhibition in the US, 1957 to 1959," *Museum and Society*, 14(3), pp. 456–71.

Jang, Shin (2004) "Hanmal iljegangjeomgi ui gyogwaseo balhaeng jedo wa yeoksa gyogwaseo [The System of Textbook Publication and Historiography during the Late Period of the Daehan Empire and the Japanese Colonial Period]," *Yeoksa gyoyuk* [History Education], 91, pp. 1–23.

Jeon, Jae-ho (1998) *Bakjeonghui cheje ui minjokjuui yeongu* [Research on Nationalism of the Park Chung Hee Regime], Unpublished PhD thesis, Sogang University.
Jeong, Sang-woo (2001) *Joseon chongdokbu ui joseonsa pyeonchan saeob* [Government-General of Korea's Compilation Project of History of Korea], Unpublished PhD thesis, Seoul National University.
Kal, Hong (2001) *Aesthetic Constructions of Korean Nationalism: Spectacle, Politics and History*, London and New York: Routledge.
Kim, Chewon (1947) "Two Old Sila Tombs," *Artibus Asiae*, 10(3), pp. 169–92.
Kim, Chewon (1957) "Masterpieces of Korean Art in America," *Artibus Asiae*, 20(4), pp. 296–302.
Kim, Chewon (1991) *Gyeongbokgung yahwa* [Gyeongbokgung Palace Nights Story], Seoul: Tamgudang.
Kim, Chewon (1992) *Bangmulgwan gwa hanpyeongsaeng* [Museum and My Whole Life], Seoul: Tamgudang.
Kim, Chewon and Kim Lena Lee (1974) *Arts of Korea*, Tokyo: Kodansha International Ltd.
Kim, Gi-su (1877) *Ildonggiyu* [Record of a Journey to Japan].
Kim, Han-gyu (1999) *Hanjung gwangyesa* [The History of the Korean-Chinese Relations], 1, Seoul: Arke.
Kim, In-deok (2009) "Chōsen sōtokubu hakubutsukan [The Government-General Museum]," in National Museum of Korea (ed.) *Hanguk bangmulgwan baknyeonsa* [The 100 Year History of Korean Museums], Seoul: Sahoepyeongnon, pp. 82–147.
Kim, K. C. (2005) *Korea as Seen through Its Material Culture and Museums*, Unpublished PhD thesis, University of Leicester.
Kim, Sang-yeop (2013), "Hanguk geundae ui misul sujangga [Art Collectors of Modern Korea]," in Seongbuk Museum of Art (ed.) *Widaehan yusan jeon* [The Great Heritage], Seoul: Seongbuk Gurip Misulgwan, pp. 104–11.
Kim, Won-yong (1985) *Gogohak gaeron* [Introduction to the Korean Archaeology], Seoul: Iljisa.
Kim, Yeong-mi (2011) "Oegyo munseo lul tonghaeseo bon gimdaejung napchi sageon gwa hanil yeondae ui du yuhyeong [Kidnapping of Kim Dae-jung and Two Types of South Korean-Japanese Solidarity as Seen from the Diplomatic Documents]," *Bakjeonghui sidae hanil gwangye ui jaejomyeong* [Review of South Korean-Japanese Relations in Park Chunghee's Era], pp. 57–102.
Kim, Yeong-myeong (1999) *Saero gocheo sseun hanguk hyeondaesa* [Newly Written Version of History of Korean Contemporary Politics], Seoul: Eulyumunhwasa.
Kim, Youngna (2000) "Bangnamhoe laneun jeonsi gonggan [Universal Exposition as an Exhibitionary Space: Korean Exhibition at the 1893 World Columbian Exposition, Chicago]," *Seoyang misulsa nonmunjip* [Journal of History of Western Art], 13, 2000, pp. 75–106.
Kim, Youngna (2002) "Hanguk misulsa ui taedu, go yuseop [A Luminary of Korean Art History, Goh Yu-seop: His Role and Position]," *Misulsa yeongu* [Study of Art History], 16, pp. 503–18.
Kim, Youngna (2015) *National Museum of Korea, the First Ten Years in Yongsan*, Seoul: National Museum of Korea.

Kimiya, Tadashi (2011) "Bakjeonghui jeonggwon gwa hanil gwangye [Park Chung Hee's Regime and South Korean-Japanese Relations]," in the Research Institute of Japanese Studies, Kookmin University (ed.) *Bakjeonghui sidae hanil gwangye ui jaejomyeong* [Review of South Korean-Japanese Relation in Park Chunghee's Era], Seoul: Seon-in, pp. 13–56.

Knell, Simon (2011) "National Museum and the National Imagination," in S. Knell et al. (eds.) *National Museums*, London and New York: Routledge, pp. 3–28.

Knez, Eugene I. (1997) *An American Perspective: Attempts for a Korean Cultural Renaissance*, Seoul: NMK.

Korean Overseas Information Service (1979) *Collection of the Press Articles Related to 5000 Years of Korean Art in San Francisco*, Seoul: Korean Overseas Information Service.

Kwon, Hang-ga (2008) "Misul gwa sijang [Art and Market]," in the National Institute of Korean History (ed.) *Geundae wa mannan misul gwa dosi* [Art and City that Meet with Modern Age], Seoul: Doosan dong-a, pp. 195–259.

Lee, Cheol-Sun (2006) "1950 nyeondae huban miguk ui daehan jeongchak [The US Policy toward South Korea in the Second Half of the 1950s]," in Park Jihang et al. (eds.) *Haebang jeonhusa ui jaeinsik* [New Understanding of the History around the Liberation], 2, Seoul: Chagsaesang, pp. 538–607.

Lee, Chung-ryeol (2011) *Gansong jeon hyeongpil* [Gansong, Jeon Hyeong-pil], Seoul: Gimyeongsa.

Lee, In-beom (2002) "Hanguk bangmulgwan jedo ui giwon gwa seongyeok [Origin and character of museum in Korea]," *Misulsa nondan*, 14, pp. 35–63.

Lee, Ji-won (2007) *Hanguk geundae munhwa sasangsa yeongu* [The History of Korean Modern Cultural Thought], Seoul: Hyean.

Lee, Jong-wook (2006) *Minjok inga, Gukga inga?* [Ethnic Nation? Or State?], Seoul: Sonamu.

Lee, Ki-baik (1961) *Hanguksa sillon* [A New National History], Seoul: Taeseongsa.

Lee, Ki-baik (1990) *Hanguksa sillon* [A New History of Korea], Seoul: Ilchogak.

Lee, Sungsi (2004) "Joseon wangjo ui sangjing gonggan gwa bangmulgwan [Symbolic Spaces of the Joseon Dynasty and Museums]," in Lim Jie-hyun (ed.) *Guksa ui sinhwa lul neomeoseo* [Beyond the Myth of National History], Seoul: Humanist, pp. 265–95.

Lee, Sun-ja (2009) *Iljegangjeomgi gojeokjosasaeob yeongu* [Investigation Projects of Historic Remains in the Japanese Colonial Period], Seoul: Gyeonginmunhwasa.

Lee, Yeong-hun (2013) *Daehanminguk yeoksa* [The History of the Republic of Korea], Seoul: Giparang.

Lim, Jie-hyun (2004) "Guksa ui an gwa bak – hegemoni wa guksa ui daeyeonswae [National History In and Out: Hegemony & the Grand Chain of National History)," in Lim Jie-hyun (ed.) *Guksa ui sinhwa lul neomeoseo* [Beyond the Myth of National History], Seoul: Humanist, pp. 13–33.

Lin, Nancy (2016) "5,000 Years of Korean Art: Exhibitions Abroad as Cultural Diplomacy," *Journal of the History of Collections*, 28(3), pp. 383–400.

Ministry of Culture and Information (1979) *Munhwagongbo samsipnyeon* [30 Years of Culture and Information], Seoul: Ministry of Culture and Information.

Ministry of Education (1957) *Gukbo dogam* [An Illustrated Guide to National Treasures], Seoul: Ministry of Education.

Ministry of Education (1960) *Munhwajae miguk jeonsi bogoseo* [A Report on Exhibitions of Cultural Objects in the US]), Seoul: Ministry of Education.

Moon, Chang-Keuk (1994) *Hanmi galdeung ui haebu* [Anatomy of Korea–US Conflicts], Seoul: Nanam chulpansa.

National Gallery of Art et al. (1953) *Exhibition of Japanese Painting and Sculpture Sponsored by the Government of Japan*, Washington, DC: National Gallery of Art.

National Gallery of Art et al. (1957) *Masterpieces of Korean Art: An Exhibition under the Auspices of the Government of the Republic of Korea*, Washington, DC: National Gallery of Art.

NMK (1948) *Two Old Silla Tombs, Ho-u Tomb and Silver Bell Tomb* [Report of the Researchof Antiquities of the Natinal Museum of Korea], 1, Seoul: Eul-yu publishing Co.

NMK (1957) *Haeoe jeonsi gomisul jeollamhoe mongnok* [Special Exhibition: Korean National Treasures Which Will Be Exhibited in the US], Seoul: NMK.

NMK (1965) *Jinyeolpum dogam* [Selected Museum Exhibits] 1945–1965, Seoul: NMK.

NMK (1968) *Cheongdong yumul dorok* [Selected Bronze Objects of the Early Metal Period in Korea 1945–1968], Seoul: NMK.

NMK (1972) *Gungnip jungang bangmulgwan* [The National Museum of Korea], Seoul: NMK.

NMK (2006) *Gungnip jungang bangmulgwan yuksipnyeon* [60 Years of the National Museum of Korea], Seoul: NMK.

NMK (2009) *Hanguk bangmulgwan bangnyeonsa jaryopyeon* [The 100-Year History of Korean Museums], Seoul: Sahoe pyeongnon.

Office of Cultural Properties (1974) *Hanguk gomisul* [Korean Ancient Art], Seoul: Gwangmyeong chulpansa.

Oh, Myeong-seok (1998) "1970~1980 nyeondae ui munhwa jeongchaek gwa minjokmunhwa damnon [Cultural Policies and Discourse on the Ethnic National Culture during the 1960s and the 1970s]," *Bigyomunhwa yeongu*, 4, pp. 121–52.

Oh, Yeong-chan (2006) *Nangnanggun yeongu* [A Study on Nangnang Commandery], Seoul: Sagyejeolchulpansa.

Pai, Hyung Il (2001) "The Creation of National Treasures and Monuments: The 1916 Japanese Laws on the Preservation of Korean Remains and Relics and their Colonial Legacies," *Korean Studies* 25(1), pp. 72–95.

Pai, Hyung Il (2013) *Heritage Management in Korean and Japan: The Politics of Antiquity & Identity*, Seattle: University of Washington Press.

Park, Chan-seung (2010) *Minjok, Minjokjuui* [Nation and Nationalism], Seoul: Sohwa.

Park, Chung Hee (1963) *The Country, the Revolution and I*, Seoul: Hyangmunsa.

Park, Gwang-hyeon (2009) "Sikminji joseon gwa bangmulgwan ui jeongchihak [The Colony Joseon and the Politics of the Museum]," in Park Gwang-hyeon (ed.) *Bangmulgwan ui jeongchihak* [Politics of Museum], Seoul: Nonhyeong.

Park, Gwang-mu (2010) *Hanguk munhwa jeongchaeknon* [Cultural Policy in Korea], Seoul: Gimyeongsa.

Park, Hyeon-su (1998) "Hangukmunhwa e daehan ilje ui sigak [The Japanese Imperialist Perspective on Korean Culture]," *Bigyomunhwa yeongu* [Comparative Study of Culture], 4, pp. 35–77.

Park, Sang Mi (2010) "The Paradox of Postcolonial Korean Nationalism: State-Sponsored Cultural Policy in South Korea, 1965-present," *Journal of Korean Studies*, 15(1), pp. 597–632.

Park, So-hyeon (2004) "Jeguk ui chuimi [Hobby of Empire: the YHM and Museum Policy of the Empire of Japan]," *Misulsa nondan* [Art History Forum], 18, pp. 143–69.

Parmar, Inderjeet (2012) *Foundations of the American Century: The Ford, Carnegie, & Rockefeller Foundations in the Rise of American Power*, New York: Columbia University Press.

Robinson, Michael E. (1988) *Cultural Nationalism in Korea*, Seattle: University of Washington Press.

Robinson, Michael E. (1990) "Forced Assimilation, Mobilization, and War," in C. J. Eckert et al. (eds.) *Korea Old and New: A History*, Seoul: Ilchogak Publishers, pp. 327–46.

Roe, Jae-ryung (1995) *The Representation of National Identity in Korean Art Exhibitions*, Unpublished PhD thesis, New York University.

Sekino, Tadashi (1904) *Kankoku kenchiku chōsa hōkoku* [Report on Investigation of Korean Architecture], Tokyo: Tokyo Imperial University, Engineering College.

Sekino, Tadashi (1910) "Kankoku geijutsu no hensen ni tsuite [On the Transition of Korean Arts]," *Chōsen*, 4(5), pp. 40–5.

Sekino, Tadashi (1932) *Chōsen bijutsusi* [A History of Korean Art], Seoul: Chosen sigakukai.

Sekino, Tadashi (1941) *Kankoku no kenchiku to geijutsu* [Architecture and Art of Korea], Tokyo: Iwanami shoten.

Seo, Joong-Seok (2007) *Korean Nationalism Betrayed*, Folkestone, UK: Global Oriental.

Shin, Gi-Wook (2006) *Ethnic Nationalism in Korea: Genealogy, Politics, and Legacy*, Stanford: Stanford University Press.

Smith, Anthony D. (1971) *Theories of Nationalism*, London: Duckworth.

Smith, Anthony D. (1991) *National Identity*, Harmondsworth: Penguin Books.

Smith, Anthony D. (2009) *Ethno-Symbolism and Nationalism: A Cultural Approach*, London and New York: Routledge.

Surak, Kirstin (2013) *Making Tea, Making Japan: Cultural Nationalism in Practice*, Stanford: Stanford University Press.

Tokyo National Museum et al. (1976) *Kankoku bijutsu gosennen* [5000 Years of Korean Art], The Asahi Shimbun Company.

Yi Royal Household Museum (1912) "Shogen [Preface]," in *Liōke hakubutsukan shojōhin shasinchō* [Catalogue of the Yi Royal Household Museum Collection], Seoul: YHM.

Yu, Hong-jun (1993) *Naui munhwayusan dapsagi* [My Essays on the Exploration of Cultural Heritage], 1, Seoul: Changjak gwa bipyeongsa.

Index

Note: Numbers in italic denote figures.

For Product Safety Concerns and Information please contact our EU representative GPSR@taylorandfrancis.com
Taylor & Francis Verlag GmbH, Kaufingerstraße 24, 80331 München, Germany

www.ingramcontent.com/pod-product-compliance
Lightning Source LLC
LaVergne TN
LVHW010926110826
845149LV00013B/2499

* 9 7 8 1 0 3 2 1 7 5 5 2 2 *